BONANZA BITS

BONANZA BITS

Discovering the Mother Lode of Everyday Savings

JOSEPH R. TRUDEL

Writers Club Press
San Jose New York Lincoln Shanghai

Bonanza Bits
Discovering the Mother Lode of Everyday Savings

Writers Club Press
an imprint of iUniverse.com, Inc.

For information address:
iUniverse.com, Inc.
5220 S 16th, Ste. 200
Lincoln, NE 68512
www.iuniverse.com

ISBN: 0-595-19013-8

Printed in the United States of America

To All The Early Pioneers Who Still Believe
In The Greatness Of America
And The Free Enterprise System

Consider the present, neither as a reflection of the past,
nor as the envied promise of tomorrow
But rather, as the opportunity to enhance society
for the benefit of all

—Joseph R. Trudel

Contents

▼

Introduction

▼

"FAN ESSENTIALS" is an opening day sports article which details the pricing structure of the Oakland Raiders football team. According to the news story, 'Seasons Tickets' range from $410 to $770—depending on seat location. Likewise, individual game tickets are shown within the $40–$80 price range. Parking fees are listed as $10 per car, $20 for RV's. Add in the cost for a couple of hot dogs, beers, peanuts, and soda (plus of course a souvenir...or two...or three), and you come away with a price tab of almost $400 just for a family of four...for a one hour performance. Compliments of the NFL, the beer and soda companies, and the other licensed manufacturers approved by the league and its teams.

Is that price worth its entertainment value? To those who attend that special event 'yes'—but for the rest of us—no way. I mean $400 for an hours entertainment? Hmmm...well, let's see what else $400 might buy instead. How about a new 27" Color TV set, which will last an average of ten years and also allow you to watch numerous games over the decade from the comfort of your own easy chair—rather than some plastic seating pad which you often need to provide for yourself, while at the game. And don't forget, that by watching the game on TV you also take a 'pass' on both the traffic and parking problems as well.

You say your hungry?…then how about having a sizzling steak at home as opposed to a cold 'hot' dog at the game—and for far less money? Once again, its totally possible if you choose wisely. Now as for those soda's and beers that are coupled with a $20 tab, let me simply say these two words—'No Way'. Reason: With your own 'home-style' version they can be had for just a few dollars at most. Bottom line—One man's priority is clearly another man's choice. And that (ie 'priority') is what determines more than anything else, our true standard of living regarding the personal satisfaction that one gets from being at a 'live performance' as opposed to watching that same game (also 'live')—but on a TV set instead. Sure the old saying of 'actually being there' has some merit—but you need to ask yourself at what price? Clearly only you can decide that—which is precisely what you must do for all purchases.

By so doing, you are essentially asking yourself if the product or service is a desired WANT or an actual NEED.

However saving money is only one component of what we need to be concerned with if we as consumers are to improve our own financial lifestyles. For clearly, just as important are the ever enhanced components of both value and good customer service. Think about this. If you forsake that morning Starbucks coffee at $4 every workday, that's $20 a week. Multiply that times the standard annual fifty work week, and you'll have $1000 tax-free dollars in less than a year. Now carry the same idea to that fast (or is it FAT?) food lunch and soon you'll have $2000 saved—enough to create a savings/investment plan that will make you feel (and look) ten times better than either that cup of 'specialty' coffee or even that so-called fast food 'value' meal.

American consumers are indeed fortunate to have so many choices in the marketplace. Yet many of us fail to think about the money-saving alternatives to many popular brand names—and as a result, we end up spending far more money than is necessary to satisfy not only our wants, but our basic needs as well.

It is a known fact that while many people earn high salaries, they never seem to have any money—while others, who make far less, somehow always seem to possess cash. The reason for this is simple: the former is a careless spender, while the latter seeks out true value for his money. (Consequently, the former explains why America has one of the lowest saving rates in the industrial world.)

Now considering the fact that 'time equals money' you might think that is simply not worth the time to comparison shop. Well...think again! If you make $20,000 a year and shop wisely, that same money will be worth at least $30,000—guaranteed!. Therefore, think about your spending as an investment, as the more you can stretch every dollar, the more you will have for items you would have normally had to take out an 18% loan for.

Clearly, the American free marketplace today is among the best classrooms of the world, since consumer protection, by itself will not protect you in all your purchasers. Rather, you alone will need to take full responsibility for where your hard-earned money goes. If you spend carelessly, and then claimed you were falsely 'ripped-off', then whose fault is that? Don't automatically always point to the seller...after all, he's in business to make a legitimate profit. Instead look in the mirror and see yourself as the one who clearly could of prevented the problem in the first place. Obviously, nobody made you buy that product, rather it was your own choice. Bottom line: to decide between one merchant over another is your choice. Likewise, the resulting cost/benefit is yours also.

Priorities then are something nobody but you can put a price one. If you think that the Super Bowl is worth $500 (or even more), so be it. After all, it's your money, so always enjoy it anyway you like. If however you wish that you had the cash for something more meaningful to you, then maybe the time has finally come for you to take full control over your own financial life.

In the following pages, you will learn some tried and true techniques for getting the most out of every dollar you spend. For example, the sound alternative of buying one brand over another will eventually amount to big bucks—believe it or not. Of course, the issue of 'quality' (as always), will be a major consideration in your choice, as well. Ironically, in many cases, that lower priced item will also be of better quality than that of its higher priced counterpart. This is not surprising, especially when you consider the exorbitant cost of advertising—especially during an event as 'hyped' as the Super Bowl is. Sure, advertising helps to sell products and services, yet the medium used (ie newsprint vs. TV), has a direct relation on the final cost of that product. Sometimes however, such costly advertisement benefits the consumer, as when the dealer offers a special promotion (ie two-for-one) in order to increase volume sales. However, most of the time, advertising clearly results in a higher cost for you. Accordingly, consumers truly need to become more aware of their own financial outgo. For with knowledge of the competitive marketplace, each of us can vastly improve our own lifestyle,—just remember that the choice to do so, is always yours. Hopefully, by the time you finish reading this book, you will have discovered several ways to stretch your hard earned dollars for living well—by simply living on less.

Chapter 1

▼

Why So Many Americans Are Such Poor Money Managers

Traditionally many Americans learn eventually how to sell both products and services, yet few of us give as much consideration on how to buy things. Therefore, it is not surprising that normally the most persuasive motivation to our buying habits is Advertising....'Madison Ave Mythology'...'Hype'...Puff. Call it what you will, but the same basic premise of the word Advertising remains simply this—to create a demand for the sellers product/service in order for him to increase sales, and thus his profits. Those profits in turn, will also increase the need for employees and thus increases the overall employment opportunities in todays economy, as well. As a result, in the end everyone seems to economically benefit to one degree or another. This is also the foundation of our economy and as such mirrors the economic dependency of seller to buyer—and vice versa.

Although good advertising should inform us, too often, it instead attempts to deceive us. A case in point is the so-called 'Cola Wars' recently waged by Coca Cola and Pepsi. One company merely claims that "It's the Real Thing" while the other boasts its product is "The Choice of A New Generation". Big Deal—so what? How about telling me instead what your product taste like. Does it have a unique taste? Describe it to me. How sweet tasting is it? What flavor does your soda have that the other doesn't? This is what the consumer really wants to know—rather than some self-described sales slogan (or jingle) thats intentionally tied to a highly paid endorsement of some noted sports celebrity. Yet, always remember what the purpose of the advertisement is—to sell the product, and NOT to give you information which may help you to think for yourself in todays marketplace. Well, that 'think for yourself' concept is exactly what you need to do every time you part with those hard-earned dollars. So the next time you have an 'urge' for a cola product, you might try giving the local store brand a 'try-out' instead. Usually you will find the price is less than the name brand, and often times even better in both the taste and quality of its ingredients.

The reason for this is simple—in that, a store puts its own reputation on the line every time it offers its own brand to the buying public. So a bad-tasting cola for example, is likely to discourage that consumer from trying another product under that same store label. The bottom line is this—there is simply too much at risk for the store to lose by offering a poorly performing product, and as such, many of these stores have their own formulas for many of its own products.

The second reason for the lower selling price is because there is no real extra (advertising) expense behind the promotion of the product. Since the store normally produces a weekly sales flyer anyway, 'X' amount of advertising space needs to be filled regardless, of whatever the product is thats being promoted thru the local media outlet (ie direct advertising or newspapers), as opposed to a national sales campaign. Of course, the cost difference between the two is reflective in the price you pay at the checkout counter. Once again, that choice is clearly yours.

Now if you were to carry that same premise of name brand vs. store brands to all your expenditures the result would likely become a real eye-opening experience to your own ego that henceforth always told you, that you were in fact, an educated consumer. Still don't believe it?—then take your own test of any one product for a month—and then see the result for yourself. Only you can judge the findings, my real suggestion here is that you merely give it a try. Bottom line: valuable dollars that could be used for savings and or investments are instead being spent on the 'puff' costs from Madison Avenue. Is it any wonder then, why many Americans continue to be such poor money managers?

Advertising however is merely an outlet thats used to entice consumers to buy. Far more important is the total lack of consumer education by both ourselves and the governments own public school system. Even today, there tends to be very few courses offered in the subject of consumer education in K-12 grade school. Yet, these students have an enormous amount of money to spend from the income they usually receive from part-time jobs and full time employment during the summer months. In time, many of these consumers will qualify for their own credit cards, yet chances are, they won't fully understand the terms and long-term obligations, which come from the cards use.

Certainly it would be far better to expose teenagers to financial services and personal money management early on in life—since after all, that process will be lifelong and would likely instill financial discipline in the early years as well—(translation: a higher standard of living!) As for the process for getting such classes into the public school curriculum, parents themselves must simply demand it, until it is finally part of the schools program.

Thus, attending the local school board meetings is a good time to present your desire to see such a course adopted. Sure you will meet opposition, but so what. If its important enough for you to make the initial proposal, then you and the others should certainly follow-thru with an appropriate action plan. Contact state legislators, write the media, and network with like minded individuals. In fact, you might even want to run for the school board yourself. The main thing is to keep active until your goal is fulfilled. Someday your children might even thank-you for doing exactly that.

Certainly, we as adults, could also use some motivation when it comes to personal money management. Case in point: We can all learn about investments by watching financial programs, or reading money magazines, or listening to financial advice on the radio. The marketplace for such information is widely available throughout this country, yet so few consumers take advantage of such opportunities, as a way to learn these financial basics for themselves. As a result, Americans now owe billions of dollars in personal debt to the banking industry, to the tune of an average18% interest rate. So here again, consumer education is the key to turning the situation around.

Now lets look at a routine buying decision: which is, shopping to buy a car? Let me ask you: what do you think you should consider even before you stepped into a car dealers showroom? Not sure? Then what you need to do is to ask yourself the following: What size car do I want/need? How much can I afford to spend? Who will likely lend me the money? If the car is financed, at what rate will the loan be set at?

Now consider this—Have you check the cars rating and repair history to be sure, that the vehicle isn't a 'lemon'? What about the cost to register and insure it? Has there been any government or manufacturer recalls on the car? Is the car a gas guzzler or an economy champ?…and perhaps most important of all—is the car reliable?

Now apply that same criteria to used cars as well. But in this case, getting an independent mechanics professional opinion is paramount towards increasing the odds for you, in obtaining a good (no make that a super) deal. Sure that diagnostic charge will likely cost you $100 or so, but at least you will have discovered the cars good and bad points , rather than eventually being surprised by your 'dream' cars constant failures and associated expensive repair bills.

Bottom line: Since buying any car today costs several thousands dollars, don't be penny-wise and pound foolish, by skimping on information regarding the cars condition, its mechanical history—or even its previous maintenance records. After all, buying anything THAT expensive without such knowledge is simply a gamble at best. At its worst, it can become a financial albatross to your own financial well-being. Thus, by playing your 'buying cards' correctly, you'll easily come out on top.

"Service" today, represents the largest expense to purchasers of related consumer products. Yet few consumers think about the cost to operate an appliance, the cost to repair a computer, or believe it or not, the expense of home repairs, even though all of these will collectively become some of the most expensive items most of us will undoubtedly encounter over the years. Yet, something like home repairs can be planned for, much easier than such immediate services, like car maintenance or even a VCR repair. So what do you look for when you need a service contractor? Who would you pick—and why?

If your surprise answer is simply to simply scan the yellow pages, you'll likely see many ads there citing the merits of each. Obviously, you'll need to spend valuable time if you plan on calling several dealers. However, there's a better way—simply ask a friend for a referral. Otherwise 'shop around' by asking each company what warranty service is provided, what the estimate of repair cost is likely to be, and how soon they can stop by and do the repair. Note: Some firms that advertise a low price, often times gives that same job, the lowest priority, when it comes to service call priority. Also don't be misled by any unbelievable 'low prices' for service. That '$20 'immediate repair' advertisement is sometimes merely a 'lure' so as to get you to contact them in the first place. Yet, once they arrive at your home, be prepared for the likely extra charges for additional repairs, of which you weren't even aware of. And so it goes-buyer beware! For with knowledge of the marketplace (and this book) you will then put the financial odds clearly in your own favor, by thus making the wisest purchasing decisions possible.

Another reason as to why Americans are such poor money managers, lies in their belief that rules and regulators from some distant, faceless bureaucracy will somehow protect us, from being ripped off. Sure, we've all heard how consumer pioneer Ralph Nader exposed General Motors in the 1960's regarding that companies 'unsafe' product—the Chevy Corvair automobile. Yet how often have you picked up the daily newspaper only to read that a woman is suing a restaurant because the coffee they served her was too hot, and as a result she burned herself? Excuse me, but why is that the companies fault?—I mean, in all those year of doing business nobody else ever complained about the product. Now could it be that there are people out there who are simply all too eager to take advantage of such lenient product liability laws? Well if you answered yes, then guess who pays for the final court judgment? Yep, that's right—the consumer—that's you and me, whenever and wherever we buy that companies product.

So consider that 'payout' of the higher retail price as simple payback for the companies cost of litigation. Nothing more, nothing less. Now do you remember the so-called massive billion dollar lawsuit against 'Big Tobacco'? Well guess what, the price of that product was ultimately raised by those same tobacco companies in order to pay off the publics claim. In other words, the smokers themselves—not the tobacco companies ended up funding their very own claim. Bottom line: Deception is often the tool used by government regulators to pacify the publics concern, while in reality, they offer very little in the way of resolution in solving the issue.

Here again, it is you the consumer who holds the winning hand. Want to penalize a company? It's simple—don't but their product. If enough of your peers try this, the company will either change its product line or simply be forced out of business. Historically, there are many companies which over the years, have done exactly that—because they did not listen to their own customers needs. Remember Atari Computer? Woolworth? Ipana toothpaste? American Motors? At one time or another each of those companies were once 'kingpins' in their own sector. Then better products from competitors came along and forced them out of the marketplace. This didn't take a law, but rather only a decision by consumers to exercise their preference in the marketplace. That is the free enterprise system at work—not some government regulation designed to hamstring corporations while enriching the legal profession with constant lawsuits, which always seems to result in higher prices to the marketplace. Accordingly, it is no secret then, that nearly two-thirds of our GNP (Gross National Product) is derived directly from consumer spending. Clearly, you and I decide the products and services we both want and need. By becoming educated in our saving/spending habits each of us can change our personal financial lifestyle for the better. That is precisely why this book was written—to inform and educate, so that you will learn how to become a smarter consumer in todays marketplace.

Why everyone must change their spending habits Remember when Jimmy Carter was President and we had 21% interest rates and inflation that seemed to rise daily, on even the most basics of living expenses? Those of us who worked two jobs just to make ends meet, now realize that saving money at the local bank was not necessarily the best way to come out ahead financially. Far better (and wiser) would it had been, to shop better by simply allowing each company to compete for your own hard-earned dollars.

Accordingly, always remember that rising interest rates also equal rising prices in todays marketplace. After all somebody has to pay, and you know that it won't be just the seller who has already taken on the financial risk, via starting his own business. Consumers, on the other hand have a self-interest in making sure that they get the most value for their dollars.

Where these two (buyer and seller) meet—when a sale is made—is in fact, the reason why our economy is today, the envy of the free world.

But lets get even more basic by saying that rising wages equals rising prices and vice versa. Accordingly, it sometimes may even appear that this pursuit is a financial 'merry-go-round', that somehow still never really seems to stop. Yet,today you can get off this monetary 'charade', simply by taking control of your own financial life. Sure we'll always have inflation, but thru wise buying habits, you personally can eliminate it from your life. How?…Thats easy, when prices rise is one area, offset it by getting more value for your money by shopping elsewhere. For example, when gas prices rise at the pump 30% or more, do you shop around in other sectors of the economy (like car insurance) to get a lower rate and thus wipe out that gas increase? If not, then clearly you should.

That in fact, is just one way of how to stay ahead of these ever changing financial conditions. So always consider alternatives. They're usually present, while just waiting for you to take advantage of them.

Heres more 'proof'—do you think that movie prices are too high at $9 a 'pop'? If so, then try the $2 matinee…or better still, rent the video at one-third the price of a first run movie. The bottom line is you can change you spending habits quite easily, in order to not only get off that financial'merry-go-round', but you can actually get ahead and live better by simply making better use of what you already have—no matter how much—or how little—that is.

Of course, any pay raise or other income you'll get will be just an illusion and short lived, if you spend it without thinking about its true (and thus, potential) value. So always ask yourself, is this item/service a want or a need? If its the former, always think twice as to how many work hours you will need to acquire the money, in order to pay for it. Now, if its the latter, simply ask yourself if there are cheaper choices which are available. In most cases, there clearly might be.

Chapter 2

▼

What exactly is a 'Bonanza Bit' ?

Readers of various consumer publications have often heard the term 'Best Buy', which basically means a quality product at a reasonable price—yet is also relative to a competing product. A 'Bonanza Bit' however, goes beyond just getting value. It also includes many common sense tactics that can save you time, spare you aggravation, and increase your own consumer awareness, whenever and wherever you happen to be.

In so doing, you won't always need to refer to some consumer rating publication—rather you will instead know what to look for—as well as what to avoid—in practically all of your buying decisions. A simple example of this would be when your purchasing 'no-name' tires, based solely on the tires sidewall ratings of temperature, traction, and tread wear. To put it bluntly: it is not really necessary to buy a brand-name tire at a higher price, since your best value would likely come from comparing the various tire ratings to each other. (The 'real' price difference however, might show up in the manufacturers warranty.) Accordingly, many other 'generic' products often fall under this premise—yet recent reports have found that off-brands often perform about as well its name brand counterpart. Still lots of people prefer the name brand, perhaps as a feeling of security, (and of course, via the bias of Madison Avenue ad agencies). My personal feeling is that you should always try the lower-priced version of an item and then if your not satisfied with it, simply 'buy-up' to the next pricier version. Its a fact, that by doing so…you will certainly save some big bucks over the long-haul. This money if invested wisely, will then give you an even higher standard of living, as well.

Throughout this book, I have inserted many money-saving suggestions—and various 'Bonanza Bits' (a total of some nifty fifty 'Bits' of information and ideas) that will help you to get more value for your hard-earned money.) You can think of these 'numerical nuggets' as perhaps being small in appearance—yet represents a true mother-lode of benefits, that is certain to increase your own standard of living.

Accordingly, the other chapters of this book goes even further, by giving you valuable information on how to get the most value on major expenses, like Travel, Investing, Taxes, Entertainment, and even Educational costs.

Clearly, once you've acquired your own knowledge of consumer education in the marketplace, you will then confidently believe in your own bargaining ability, and thus not have to rely on some slick marketing slogan to decide your own buying decision for you. (I speak from experience having grown up as a thrift Yankee in value-conscious New England.)

Heres one more thing, before we get started—never solely rely on others (ie consumer protection agencies, advertising, and sales pamphlets) to help you with your buying patterns. In reality, only you have the total power (i.e. via moneys purchasing power) to determine if all these entitys even exist. If you buy wisely (via consumer education), you won't need the 'hype' from the ad agencies nor the bloated bureaucracy of government agencies to solve a problem, that, in reality will no longer even exist—for you. Now just think for a moment about that acquired surge of consumer confidence—and then read on!

Bonanza Bit #1—Your best value for buying beverages comes from making home-brewed tea. Not only is it better tasting, it also is healthier for you as well. Pour some over ice and you have a refreshing drink for just pennies (vs, paying $2 at many restaurants).

Eureka! I've found 'Bit#2'—Looking for a cheap form of entertainment for the family? Well, instead of joining the crowds to Disneyland, opt instead for the County Fair. Here you'll get interesting exhibits, tasty food, and often times free entertainment (a'la live band) all for the price of just a few dollars—and thats for the whole family!

Ya…hoo! You've prospected and discovered Bit#3—Prepaid Phone Cards which can save you some big BUCKaroos when you need to make a phone call while your away from home. Not only will the per minute rate be less than what a pay phone would cost, it will also be more convenient—in that, you'll never have to be concerned with having the correct change.

A true Diamond in the Dust—Bit#4—This 'Diamond' comes in the shape of a disposable camera. At $5 a pop you won't have to worry about losing that precious $150 (35MM) keepsake. Sure the pictures won't be as great, but for most people (and consumer testing labs), its value cannot be matched. (I've tried several brands all which gave very good to excellent pictures.)

Bit#5 Return to Sender?—No, not if you enjoy saving 33% off your postage costs simply by sending a postcard at .20 vs. .34 for a letter. Sure you can't send the same amount of information, but their perfect for requesting information,…and also don't forget to bring some .20 stamps on your next vacation, for mailing picture postcards as well.

Bit#6 You light up my life…simply by having a 2 D-Cell flashlight. In fact, buy two of them. One for the home and the other for the car. At $1 (or less) you'll find it really comes in handy when the lights go out at home or when your car breaks down in the middle of the night. Also be sure to always use alkaline batteries for the longest storage life.

Bit#7 Quicksilver—Think of the bicycle as a clean, efficient, and a low cost form of transportation. Today. you can get a quality made 'hybrid' bike for less than $300. If you think that costs too much, then just think about all the money you waste on costly gas while driving to the local convenience store. An extra benefit comes from the exercise you get. (Overall, a bicycle is a 'best buy' in every sense of the term.)

Bit#8 Action Line—Been ripped off lately, and don't know where to turn to? Well then, just pick up you local newspaper and see if they offer a Consumer Action Line. If so, then be sure to contact them. Chances are, they'll at least start the resolution ball rolling towards solving your complaint. True, you still might need to take your complaint to a small claims court, but with official letterhead correspondence from the Action Line, your case will undoubtedly be all the more convincing to the judge.

Bit#9 Copycat—Making copies of all your important papers, credit cards, and documents can save a lot of aggravation and expense, in the event that the originals get either lost of destroyed. Most copy outlets charge .05 a copy—which is much cheaper than paying for a duplicate from the original source—(ie such as a bank,which would likely charge you $1.50—or more).

Bit#10 Box-Office Tickets—Want to save a few dollars the next time you want to go and see a live concert? Well, rather than paying up to an additional $10 for using the service of a ticket agency, purchase the tickets yourself via the box-office. (Chances are you'll also get a better selection of seats as well.)

Bit#11 Clean Water—Don't pay 'big-bucks' for great tasting water. Instead make your own via buying a water filter and installing it yourself. For just pennies, you'll get magnificent tasting water—without the high cost of the many bottled brands. Here's an additional benefit, the next time you do buy a small bottle of 'famous name water', save the empty container and fill it with your own 'home-brewed' version. You'll clearly impress others, while some saving money as well.

Bit#12   City Maps—Ever tried to find a street simply by asking strangers for directions? If so, you'll soon discover the benefit of having a local map instead. For just a few dollars, you'll get from point A to B without wasting valuable time (via asking others—and hoping that their information is in fact, correct.)

Bit#13   Lotto tickets—(Make that a 'lucky #13'). It's true…even if you have several losing lotto tickets you can deduct these from any winnings (a necessary requirement) on your itemized income tax form. So who knows, maybe you'll someday hit the 'Big One'—and then get to keep just a little bit more…than you might have otherwise.

Bit#14   Flea Markets—Looking for a way to turn trash into cash? Well heres a sure-fire answer—simply take all you unneeded and unwanted goods to the local flea market. For just a few dollars fee (for a rental stall), you'll have the opportunity to present your goods to several hundred potential buyers…all in just a few hours.

Bit#15   Rainchecks—Have you ever driven all over town to buy an item that was on advertised as being on sale, only to find it was already sold-out? Then next time, simply ask for a rain check—especially if its on a big-ticket item like a TV or some other major appliance. This store-issued 'I.O.U.' will basically guarantee you the same sale price for up to 1 month in most cases.

Bonus: some stores may even offer you an additional10% discount as extra compensation for your own inconvience.

Bit#16   Ear Plugs—This is something I found out about the hard way. At both a concert and the movie theater, the sound volume is usually cranked up so loud, that you'll literally sometimes wish you had a set of ear plugs in order to protect your hearing. Don't worry, even if you use them, you'll still be able to hear the sounds at both locations quite comfortably. So for just a few dollars, why not save your precious hearing, by bringing along the ear plugs—just in case. (Better safe—than sorry!)

Bit#17   Credit Balance—I know,…I know…is he kidding? He wants me to carry a credit balance to the tune of 20% or more. Not at all.

However, if your balance is less than the amount due thats required to avoid interest charges, then why not get two important benefits: First, you can get extra interest by merely keeping that money in your own credit union (or bank) account and second, you'll save on the additional cost of postage, since you won't be mailing in the additional payment a month or so before its required. Just make certain that once the credit balance exceeds this minimum amount due, you send in the full payment to avoid all interest charges.

Bit#18 Home Equity Loans—Want a personal loan but without the usual high interest rate attached to it? Then apply for a Home-Equity Loan. If you itemize your taxes, the interest charge will likely become a tax-deduction—thus cutting the loans 'true' interest rate by your own tax-rate. Warning: Do not however, take such a loan if you have any doubt that you'll be unable to pay it back. Otherwise, you could lose your own home, which is in fact, used as collateral for the loan.

Bit#19 Quartz Wristwatch—Is it a Rolex (type) or a Timex? Well according to some consumer testing organizations, both watches share one important component—accuracy. So if that's your #1 reason for buying a watch, buy the least expensive brand—and invest the extra thousand dollars towards something that's truly worthwhile.

Bit#20 Small Cars—High m.p.g. (miles per gallon), low maintenance costs, and reasonable insurance rates make such cars both practical and dependable transportation—especially if most of your driving is in the city. True, these cars are not as safe as some larger vehicles, but the fact is, their are quite practical for many urban drivers. After all, when was the last time that you really NEEDED (there's THAT word again) a SUV to go from one block to the other ? Clearly most people don't—so why, pay for it?

Bit#21 Sweepstakes Entries—Talk about a long shot. Yes, the odds are certainly against you ever hitting the so-called 'Big Enchilada' of contests. So the next time your feel lucky, why not gamble instead on a sweepstakes entry (via a postage stamp,) rather than buying some extremely 'long-shot' lotto ticket? Either way your chances are really about the same—the difference lies in the cost–34 for postage vs. $1 for a ticket (A price difference of 67%)!

Bit#22   Extended Warranties—(Sometimes)—It has long been assumed that such warranties are a waste of money—and overall they are—unless you happen to need one, at a time when your least likely to have the funds to pay for the products repair. Of course, here I'm referring to some large ticket items—like a car or a big-screen TV, which possibly has a history of unreliability. In which case, the pricier extended warranty could end up saving you some serious money. (Of course, for most lower price items, you should simply 'pass' on these warranties.)

Bit#23   'How To' Books—Want to earn $75 or more on computer repairs? If the answer is yes, then invest in a repair manual for under $15. Although you might not be so inclined as to attempt some complicated repairs, you will still save some serious money even on just ONE repair, by 'doing it yourself'. Thus your $15 book investment will have conceivably given you a tax-free return of some 500% on that labor charge. This same scenario applies to auto repairs, plumbing, and many other services, as well.

Bit#24   Pencil-type tire gauge—A good set of car tires can cost several hundred dollars, so you naturally want them to last as long as possible. One sure way to make that happen is by buying yourself a $5 tire gauge in order to make sure the tire pressure is always correct. Since both low and high pressures do result in excessive tirewear, a few dollars invested here will save you from replacing the tires prematurely. Note: don't depend on a service stations air pressure gauge—as most of them are grossly inaccurate.

Bit#25   Auto Junk Yards—Rather than automatically spending big bucks on dealer replacement parts for your car, you might instead, want to call around to the local junk yard and inquire if they have the necessary part that your car requires. If they do, then you'll most likely get the item for 75%—or less. True, the usual 30 day warranty won't be as long as when buying a new part, but chances are you'll still get a time to try the used item out. (And if the cost of the part is more than $100, then this IS the only way to go.)

Bit#26 Solar Window Film—Consider this low-cost alternative as a complement to air-conditioning, and also as an efficient way to save on 'Big Green' (ie both money and the environment). A window film that costs ($15–30) can reduce damaging UV rays by 90% or more, and will also save you from having to operate your air-conditioning more than you normally might. Try also applying this energy-efficient film to both your auto as well as your home. By adding a folding windshield sunscreen, (to be used when your cars parked) you'll certainly notice the 'cooling' difference inside. Total cost—less than $50!

Bit#27 Tax-Free States—If you live close to a state that doesn't have a sales tax, be sure to take advantage of that fact, when you vacation there. Think about it—if you spend $1000 on clothing and gifts, you'll save nearly $100 by buying in the tax-free state. (The same premise applies to counties having varying sales-tax rates within the same state.)

Bit#28 Copy Cat Art—Want a 'Rembrandt-like' painting without its expensive price tag? Then consider purchasing a print of it instead. With many of todays high-tech copying equipment, possessing such high quality (state of the) 'art' reproduction capabilities, most viewers will be unlikely to know if its real—or even if its…well…'mimic-x.'

Bit#29 Small Microwave Ovens—If your living quarter is cramped or you just don't NEED a $200 medium size 'food zapper', then buy a name-brand version for $59. It's perfect for quickly heating items up and is also cheap to operate. You'll also definitely appreciate it during the hot summers, since you won't have to light an oven.

Bit#30 Board Games—Tired of TV? Then get together with your friends to try out one of the many challenging board games thats currently available for less than $30. Now here's an added bonus: Bring it along on your next vacation,—as it will prove a viable alternative to watching those endless summer reruns.

Bit#31 Library Card—Read the current Best-Seller, hear your favorite CD, and check out recent videos—all for free, at your local library. Since your taxes fund their products and services, make sure you utilize them by applying for a free library card, the very next time you visit.

Bit#32 Sunglasses—Save both eye strain and money by purchasing 'generic' sunglasses for under $5. Not only will you get good eye protection, you'll also keep the extra $50-$100 you' would had otherwise paid for the fancy frame and the designer label.

Bit#33 Self-Help Medical Guide—For a price of $20 or so, you can get 'free' medical advice, which could save you both time and money (via not visiting the doctor). No, this won't abolish that truly necessary medical assistance from a doctor, but it will tell you what symptoms and treatments you should take for most minor illnesses. Clearly, such a guide will pay for itself, the very first time you use it.

Bit#34 AC Adapter—If you use a lot of alkaline batteries, you might want to invest in an AC power adapter—and save yourself some big-bucks over the years. Same deal applies with DC Adapters for small TV sets, (i.e. to be used when camping, for example.)

Bit#35 Recycling Aluminum Cans—At $1 a pound you can make several hundred dollars a month simply by doing this during and after the holiday season. This will also save both energy and the environment as well!

Bit#36 Early-Bird Dinners—Save 25% (at least) by eating at most restaurants before the crowded dinner hour begins—(ie. 6pm). Actually, this is a sure-fire way to cut your restaurant tab—and is also a good way to try a different culture of food, while saving you some 'big bucks' in the process

Bit#37 Free and low-costs pets—If your looking for an animal companion, be sure to check out the local 'alternative' newspaper (or Humane Society). There you'll likely find a listing of available pets for either free or low cost. In most cases, these pets comes from owners who are looking for a good home for the various small animals. The benefit here is two-fold—

as recent studies have shown that people tend to live longer and often happier, once they have a pet.

Bit#38 Running Shoes—Looking for a way to drop that extra weight? Then invest in a good pair of running shoes. They not only will serve as good exercise equipment, but will also serve as your casual walking shoes as well. Expect to pay about $40 for very good quality—which is quite reasonable when compared to other competing equipment such as a well-made bicycle or exercise treadmill.

Bit#39 Audio/Video Tapes—Now here's a 'Best Buy', if ever there was one. On sale, you can stock up on both of these for about $1 each...a price which over time, will return a hundred times that amount by giving you recorded copies of your favorite music and TV programs.

Bit#40 Internet Sales—Save on your states sales tax by buying your merchandise over the 'Net'. Sure you might have to pay for shipping & handling charges, but often times, even those charges are included in the final product price. So always check out the 'bottom-line' cost on the 'Net', before you pay extra bucks elsewhere, for the same item.

Bit#41 Nearby City Restaurants—Here's one (and mostly unknown) way to cut your eating-out tab: Eat in a nearby city where the cost of living is lower than your own town. Usually, most restaurants will want to offer you more value for the dollar, simply because their own overhead costs are lower than that of the surrounding cities.

Bit#42 December Shopping—I know...the crowds, bad traffic/parking problems, and long lines. Yet, this is the time of year when retailers do about 40% of their annual business. Translation for you: Super deals all around. The reason is simple: intense competition among retailers for your dollar.

Bit#43 Off Brand Products—Whether its tires or TV sets, you can get some excellent buys. How? By simply trying them out. In most cases, you'll soon find that one store brand is almost as good (and sometimes even better) as the national version. The price difference between the two is the result of the products brand name. So even if the name brand is somewhat better quality, ask yourself if that difference is worth the usual 200% (or greater) price difference. In most cases, it won't be.

Bit#44 Out of Town Newspaper—If your looking to rent a car in a distant city, be sure to check out the deals in that city's newspaper. True, you'll pay a premium for the paper, but you'll likely find some good rental deals listed there. Same premise applies to hotel/motel rates.

Bottom Line: Don't depend on the national chains to give you the lowest rates. Check out the 'real world' competition for yourself. 'Out of Town' paper outlets can be located in the yellow pages, as well as in most major bookstores.

Bit#45 Phone Book Discount Coupons—Looking to save some big bucks on services? Then try the phone book. In many editions, you will find a separate section that lists many discount coupons. Don't overlook these savings, some of which offer discounts of 50%—or more.

Bit#46 Happy Hour—Although these are not quite the 'best buys', they once were, some bars still offer late afternoon specials on both food and drinks. Usually for the price of a discounted drink, you'll also get a variety of free or low cost munchies. The best deals however, always seem to occur during the Monday Night Football season. Just remember to keep your drinking cost to a minimum. Otherwise, you'll end up paying more than you would might have, even at a fancy restaurant.

Bit#47 Clothesline—Want to save $100 or more a year? Then the next time you wash clothes, buy a clothesline and end forever those escalating drying costs. Each laundry dryer 'load' costs on average, $2 a week—yet for the price of just a few dollars (for the clothesline) you can 'pocket the difference.' For cold weather drying—buy a folding drying rack for under $10. Either way, your return on this 'investment' will be...eh well... 'twentyfold'.

Bit#48 Second Run Video Outlets—Just as you can save money on matinee movie tickets, you can also save on your video rental costs by patronizing retail stores that advertise rentals for $.99—or less. Although these movies may be a few months old, so what? Take pleasure in the fact, that instead of paying $9 for a new release at the multiplex theater, you can now rent 9 movies for the price of one!

Bit#49 Teaser Rate Credit Cards—You know the ones I'm talking about: "0%" interest rate for the first six months of use, then a much-higher rate (18-21%) after that. No problem—because after that initial six months expires, you simply switch to the next 'free' teaser interest rate offer. Beware however of any 'transaction charges' on a balance transfer—as this can easily cancel out your anticipated savings. Also be sure to pay your outstanding balance as much as possible to avoid the expensive habit of always paying late.

Airline Bumping—Bit#50—If your looking for some extra cash, offer to be 'bumped' voluntarily during the holiday travel season. By offering to give up your reserved airline seat, you'll get either a payment of several hundred dollars—or a free ticket for future travel. So, if your looking to cut your own travel expenses, thats one way to do it.

Chapter 3

▼

Best Buys in Todays Marketplace— Major Expenditures

America is a land of unimaginable choices when it comes to both the products and services it offers to all of us—and the world. As a result, it somehow seems ironic that so few consumers apparently seem to appreciate this fact, while the rest of the world still clamors to come here, in part, for its higher standard of living.

Still there is a wide variety of known values that many of us seem to take for granted, while yet overlooking some of the more mundane items, which we most likely see and use everyday. These items are real money savers. In fact they are 'best buys', in that these items sell for both a reasonable price while offering extra value for your money:

Here then is a list of 'Best Buys' from todays marketplace:

'2 for 1 deals'—Today you can see them quite often—especially in the grocery stores. By taking advantage of such deals its like getting a 100% 'tax-free' return on your money.

19-25" Color TV sets—for a price of $150 to $300 you can have unlimited access to the world of entertainment, sports, and public affairs. Since the average set now last some dozen years, this is truly a best buy (in fact, make that a SUPER entertainment 'best buy') in todays marketplace.

Used Cars—especially American made. I say this not to plug the domestic manufacturers, but to report the reality of the market. A used domestic auto usually sells for less than the imports and is actually made quite good when compared to foreign models. This does not necessarily mean that Ford or Chrysler products are better made than say, Toyotas, but rather that they seem to offer a better value for your money. Reliable—yes. Cheaper to insure?-Usually. Parts cheaper to buy?-Yes. Only in the area of annual depreciation do foreign cars have a value-oriented edge, but because the imported car usually costs several thousands dollars more to purchase, you'll still likely come out ahead by buying a domestic, if especially you maintain the car yourself and hold onto it for several years.

Small Claims Court—If you have a civil dispute thats not worth hiring a 'legal eagle' (ie lawyer) at $100 an hour, you can still get satisfaction at your local county court house. Sure you'll most likely need to do all the legwork and paper processing yourself, but in the end it will be just you versus your opponent. Bottom line: no attorneys are allowed to represent (or intimidate) either one of you. Today, these courts set a maximum amount that you can sued for, (usually its less than $5000), but that's still ok too. At least you'll likely get the chance for getting some restitution for the financial loss you've encounter. The usual cost for filing a claim and having papers served amounts to less than $50. (Thats not bad considering the alternative of losing everything if you can't afford an attorney.)

Community Colleges—Yes, I hate to mention it, but even junior college tuition has gone up in recent years—just as it has in all other areas of public and private education. Yet, for two years you can acquire an Associates Degree in most fields at a very reasonable cost. Although such credentials won't normally be worth as much as a Bachelors Degree in the workplace, you do win on two important points. First, you've gotten the first two years towards your Bachelors degree at a lower price than if had you gone initially to a four-year state college and Second, you now have a Associates degree in a field where you can start to build a career path, while deciding if you still want to pursue that advanced degree. Since not all high-paying jobs today require a four year degree, you might even want to consider a vocational career—such as computer repair, or plumbing, both of which do not.

Car Insurance—Think one company is the same as all the others? Don't believe it! (ie no way, no how). Just as gasoline prices vary from one station to the next, so does the price you pay for the insurance premiums on your car. Simply by shopping around among the various independent agents, and by then dealing directly with the companies themselves (rather than thru an agent), you can literally save hundreds of dollars ever year on this expense. However, one of the best ways to reduce your annual cost, is to totally drop unnecessary coverage, like collision or comprehensive— especially if your car is more than five years old. However, be certain not to 'under-insured' yourself either, especially if you have assets which could be attached by the courts once your limit of liability is exceeded.

Domestic Discount Airfares—With so much competition going on with the airlines today, you can somewhat forget about the high and low seasons when it comes to airfares. Instead concentrate on what the competition is doing. For example, how often have you been glancing thru the daily newspaper, and then spotted a 72 hour promotional fare, which is then quickly matched (or reduced even further) by yet another competitor? And I'm talking about airfares to the many popular destinations in the months of July and August. Sure you'll pay more than you would to fly during the 'gray sky' month of January, but you'll also enjoy better weather for that extra price. So if you have the desire to travel during a cities 'high-season', keep aware of such 'instant' promotions, and remain flexible, since you often need to travel within a very short time frame, in order to get that low price.

Minor League Baseball Tickets—Although many minor league sports, cost less than the "Majors", it is baseball where you are likely to save the most money—especially if you patronize the game frequently—via purchasing a 'seasons-ticket'. Think about this—if you save just $10 per game (very easy to do when you also consider the price difference for parking, hot dogs/beer, and various souvenir items) and you attend just two games a week, thats $20 (minimum) a week, $80 a month, or $480 for the usual six-month season. Your savings are actually even higher, once you add in the fact, that you'd likely receive a better seat (and at a lower cost), as a result of the general admission/box office ticket price vs. that of a major league team.

Yet even if you still opt to see a 'Major League' team, keep an eye out for the usual reduced ticket prices that seem to always emerge during the height of the summer baseball season (ie early July). Accordingly, discount coupons will often appear in the sports section of your daily newspaper. Bottom line—try never to pay full-price for such a temporary product as a baseball game. As with most items, prices usually fall when demand suddenly levels off, a promotion is introduced or worse of all (at least for the owners)—enough people, decide to stay away in large enough numbers.

Nevada—No, its not Paris or London, (nor does it pretend to be), but the cities of Las Vegas and Reno has something for just about everyone. Yet, aside from the gambling industry, their are lots of reasonably priced 'all you can eat' buffets, as well as some very interesting musical/theater presentations—the cost of which, is often included in the price of your basic hotel expense. Sure, other cities offer similar types of entertainment, but Vegas especially seems to give you more value for the dollar.

For example—Outside of this gambling mecca in the desert, you'll also find lots of other interesting sites as well—a tour of the nearby Hoover Dam, numerous and historically interesting ghost towns, the Mother Lode silver 'boom town' of Virginia City, plus many beautiful state and national parks, all of which offer everything from camping to star-gazing. Now for those of you who are of the UFO/'ET' belief, a town (Rachel) where you and your peers can gather to discuss the latest gossip of nearby 'Area 51—the often 'alleged' landing base for those alien visitors from outer space. From Vegas, you might also like to travel 'due north' as well. For here you'll discover a real 'find' in the presence of that states mining museum (located in that states capitol—Carson City), which is sure to peak your interest. (Personally, I think its one of the best in the country and recently spent a full day exploring it.) Next add in the resort area of nearby Lake Tahoe and the gaming/entertainment city of Reno, and you have one of the best vacation values around today for the money. Yet as reasonable as Nevada's cost is to the visitor, it can become even less—simply from the many discount books that appear in restaurants and hotel lobbys, throughout the state. If there is one warning however to be aware of, it is simply this—always limit the amount of money you are willing to gamble, and then stick to it. Accordingly, if you can abide by that principle, your visit to Nevada can certainly qualify as a travel 'Best Buy'.

Discount Books—you know the ones—(Entertainment Publications, in particular), which serves many urban areas—and now are available for some other countries as well. For a reasonable cost of $25 to $60, you can receive numerous coupons, which in return, are worth several thousand dollars to you, on the purchase on everything from local fast-foods outlets to several sought-after international air fares. Now if your truly the budget oriented type, yet lack the discipline to keep track of most of your expenses,than this is simply one of the best (and easiest) ways to save money today. Consider this—even if you don't use 95% of the discount coupons in the publication, you'll still come out ahead, by simply using the others. Although the books are not available to all areas of the U.S., you can still usually find one for most of our major vacation cities and/or states. Usually, the local Chamber of Commerce will offer them for sale, so always check them out first for the book as well as other 'freebie' coupons/maps. One final note: if you order a Entertainment Publications book that covers a city outside of where you live, the price is usually 25% less, than your local edition would be.

Personal Computer—Once upon a time, PC's users had an image among the public as being mindless 'nerds', who played mainly video games on their machines and very little else. Since those days, the whole image of the 'contemporary' PC user has become more mainstream, thanks in part to the "Super-Highway" of cyber space, which has since become known simply as the Internet.

Both of the major computing systems (PC/Mac's) sold today, will usually come complete with a uniform entertainment and educational package as well. A Video Card, which is usually built in the system, even allows you to turn your computer into a TV, thus sparing you the extra expense of having to buy another TV. Granted the screen size is small, yet it serves most dens or small bedrooms quite perfectly. The CD-ROM, likewise allows you to play music CD's (while working on your computer at the same time), thus once again sparing you the extra expense of having to purchase a separate CD player.

Of course, there are the other obvious benefits of owning a PC—such as sending e-mail vs. the expense of a long-distance phone call. In addition, you also have what amounts to an instant form of communication…to anyone, at anytime, to anywhere in the world. That in of itself makes a PC/Mac today a true investment, rather than simply just another household appliance. Accordingly, heres some additional benefits which are derived from having a PC:

Do you ever have a need to create printing or graphics? Well, here again, the computer can save you some 'serious' money, by allowing you to create your own preferences/style at anytime—and for any occasion (ie weddings, birthdays, graduations…etc.) Now think about this—how often have you tried to repeatedly phone someone with important information, yet were only able to get their answering machine instead? If you answered too many times too many, then heres a better way—try sending them a computer fax instead. Once you do, then chances are, they will become aware of your message much quicker than they would be from eventually playing back you voice on their phone recorder.

Still theres yet another money-saving/making benefit to a PC—which is normally not consider by the prospective buyer and that is when trading stocks? Simply by learning how to do Internet Trading yourself, you will have saved a substantial amount of money over what you would of normally had to pay a stockbroker for the same trade. So adding it all up, a PC or Mac computer certainly qualifies as a Best Buy—and then some.

Minor Expenditures to Save Even More Although the preceding major expenditures amount to big savings, here are some other items—(granted by comparison their expense is minor) that also qualify as 'best buys' in todays marketplace:

Video Rentals—are usually priced two-thirds less than a full-priced movie ticket, plus as an added 'plus' you can see the movie when YOU want, rather than when it appears at the local theater.

College Plays—Want to see Phantom of the Opera without the $100 ticket price? Then try the local community college where ticket prices are a fraction of what most 'Broadway-like' theaters would charge.

Chamber of Commerce—While there is usually no expense involve here to use its services, this can be your headquarters to find discount coupons, facts about the business community (like its tax rates), and other important information which you might need to know before starting a business in that locale. It is also a good source for making contact with other business owners and related peer groups. Bottom line: be certain not to overlook all of its valuable resources, so as to avoid spending extra time and money when obtaining similar information elsewhere.

Credit Unions—Tired of paying high 'service' fees and getting low (or zero) interest on your savings from your bank? You can easily turn the tables around, by joining your local Credit Union. Sure the savings (dividend) rate will likely be competitive of the current market conditions, but its various 'nuisance' fees (i.e. for using another branch location ATM, paying for a bounced check, or getting a copy of a statement) will likely also be less than those that are charged by the banks.

Community Museums—Many of these are free and offer some very interesting art and exhibits, yet unfortunately, most people never bother to even explore them. Clearly, these institutions should be listed as part of everyone's 'places to visit' list-even while on vacation. In addition, the frequent reviews in the local paper, clearly confirm that just because the 'artwork on display' may be from some unknown artist, that does not make such paintings/exhibits any less appealing. After all, since beauty is in the eye of the beholder, it usually pays to check them out, along with any other visiting exhibition or works display.

International Airfares—Would you believe that its often times cheaper to fly to Europe from the west coast than it is to New England? It's true. You just need to watch for those short-term promotional newspaper ads which offer international discounted fares, which usually appear during europes legendary 'shoulder season' (ie Nov-Mar). You'll also likely save big bucks on hotels at that same time, as well. Want to save even more? Then try learning the language of that country in advance of your visit. By so doing, you'll be much more likely to barter successfully when shopping there.

Ethnic Restaurants—Are you tired of the local fast food outlet from around the corner? If so, then try the nearby (and often times, 'independent') ethnic eatery. For close to the same price of that famous name 'value meal', you can have a variety of food that could even make you an frequent customer of such restaurants. For instance, just think of all the variety of food thats available today—(Mexican, Chinese, Thai, Indian, etc, etc). and you'll understand that truly the rich-tasting flavors of the world are at your command. True, you will undoubtedly like some of it—while not the others. But hey…isn't that whats life's about anyway—variety?

Public Transit—Sometimes (but not always) urban transit systems can save you both time and money, as when getting from point A to B. Yet, besides saving you that extra expense of parking fees, you'll also likely spare yourself, the emotional 'wear and tear' of driving around town in the hope of trying to find some 'unknown' location on your own. Of course, it is really during the daily 'rush hour' when you'll usually get to judge the many buses, trains, and trolleys that offer to take you elsewhere. (Yes, some systems are much superior to others.) Regrettably however, many of these transit systems also has a serious image problem which deters most of the public from using its service namely urban crime. So before you decide to 'get on board', be certain to ask the 'local's' about the the routes' 'gauntlet', it will be going thru. If it seems unsafe, opt for a taxi instead—or try joining a car pool if that trip is part of your daily commute schedule.

Camping—Ah…the great outdoors. Yes, even in America where others come far afar to see the splendor of America the Beautiful, many of us have still not explore our own 'backyards'—(i.e. the state and county campgrounds). Yet, for a nominal cost of under twenty bucks a night, 'X' number of people can pitch a tent, gaze above at the shooting stars, sing beside a roaring campfire—and enjoy that change of pace thats often derived from merely being in touch with natures glory. Sure, this whole outing will require time and effort to set up the tent, lay out your bedroll, and then set the 'dining' table, but when you add in the nearby sound of chirping crickets, a constant rushing nearby stream, and the smell/sounds of the natural habitat—you'll likely appreciate all the effort, as truly being worthwhile. For even though in recent years, many camping 'conveniences' (i.e. cable TV access, 'in-park' grocery stores) have emerged from those 'golden days of yesteryear', try instead to enjoy the great outdoors, as it was meant to be—via rustic simplicity. In essence, as a family get together, few such events are quite as enjoyable as camping is.

Rentals—How many times have you bought a product, used it once, and then had to eventually find space for it, in order for it to simply gather dust? If 'too often' is your answer, then you really need to reevaluate your own spending habits. Clearly, most of the time renting an item is a better (and usually) less expensive way to go. You can prove it yourself, here's how:—Want to take up a sport? Well, instead of spending several hundred dollars 'up-front' for the necessary equipment, try renting it instead. Then once you see yourself as becoming routinely involved in that sport, you then can start to comparison shop for the exact items you want.

In effect , by simply delaying your buying expenditures you'll win twice. First, your unspent money will continue to earn interest and second, you won't have a large financial loss should you soon decide later that you've lost your initial interest in that activity.

Estate Sales—These 'fire sales' bargains may occur for any number of reasons: (ie death, divorce, or even relocation). Yet whatever the reason, such events offer you the opportunity to save some big 'buckaroos' on just about any item you'd likely find within the homes possessions. From furniture to fancy kitchen appliances, this is your basic 'smorgasbord' towards buying many low-cost 'staples'—(and even some luxuries items, as well.) The one caution however, is simply this: know the approximate value of any item your interested in, prior to making an offer to buy it. An additional benefit: with time on your side, you'll also have the upper hand in the item's selling price. These are just a few of the literally hundreds of additional ways to save money in todays marketplace. In the following chapters you will read about savings in travel, investing, taxes, entertainment, services—and even some 'scams' to scan to avoid the bogus parting of your hard earned money.

So please read on….while you continue to enjoy the informative journey for improving your own financial well-being.

Chapter 4

▼

Travel Expenses—Hold on to your luggage…and your wallet

Perhaps no industry in the country today, is as competitive for your dollar as that of the travel industry. Yet, often times we hear about those two financial 'cringe' words ('price-fixing'), which seems to tell us, that all the hoop and holler over airfares and various travel booking requirements is merely a pricing 'charade' solely meant to deceive the commuting public. You can truly, take it from someone who has travel a great deal—the 'real deals' are really out there, just as are the con-men with their snake-oil ploys. So how then do you know which is which? Simply by understanding that ultimately, Consumer E-D-U-C-A-T-I-O-N is the key.

For instance, lets say you want to travel to the east coast to visit relatives. Assuming you are flexible as to when (and where) your willing to fly, you can save several hundred dollars—just on the basic airfare alone. Other related costs issues: Need transportation while there? If so, then you'll want to line up your rental car well in advance of the date its needed, in order to simply get the best rate possible. And so what about lodging costs? If you think you can 'wing' it and get a room, simply by showing up at the registration desk at check-in time, you need to think again? For although that still might be true in some smaller cities,it's certainly not valid with todays higher and higher occupancy rates. Accordingly, always give the word 'reservation' a priority thought whenever lodging is required. Doing so, will likely save you some big bucks (and headache) over time.

Previously, most hotels/motels had 30% or more vacancy rates during their 'off-season'. Those days are (for the most part) long gone—as witnessed by the escalating prices of even some 'budget' motel chains, which now charge $60 a night (or more) for little more than four walls, a TV, and a spartan-like shower stall. Sure I could give you the names of some lodging sites that will give your more value for your money, but far more valuable is knowing what to look for when shopping for travel services—as well as its alternatives.

What then am I referring to? Simply that you try to cut your overall travel costs 'to the bone' by logically planning ahead. "A journey of a thousand miles might begin with a single step"—but did you also know that planning your trip also requires both time and some 'heavy-duty' energy as well?

Like most well planned objectives, your results will mirror the amount of effort you put into it. Having a travel agent is sometimes a wise decision, yet you can't usually depend on him to find you the best airfare (or travel package), if his firm is only aligned with certain airlines? Far better (and more cost-effective) is for YOU to do the research (and sometimes legwork) in order to get the best deal possible. Think its not worth your time? Well if saving several hundred dollars is not appealing to you, then so be it. In the long run however, you'll gain valuable knowledge over several things: First you will have taken complete control of your own travel savings plan. Second, you will begin to understand how the airlines, hotels, and car rental agencies survive financially—and how you can then turn around those same financial tables—in your own favor. And finally, you will have developed an inner sense of what travel pitfalls to avoid (as well as which ones to profit from) simply by becoming more knowledgeable of exactly where your own travel dollars go.

Now to begin with, let's first look at the most critical aspect of any travel plan—and that is, well...you guess it...MONEY. Of course, it would be nice to go anywhere or wherever you want, but basic economics (a'la Economics 101) clearly dictates otherwise. Yet once a $ figure is arrived at, you can then start to figure out, how to s-t-r-e-t-c-h each and every dollar for its 'Maximum return. And no...I'm not talking about taking 'red-eye flights', eating your meals in your own hotel room, or (gulp!) renting a sub-compact 'toy', when you desires clearly cry out for a greater upscale alternative. Rather, you will be acquiring the financial 'know-how', in order to make your travel dreams a viable reality.

And so initially, you will want to plan out how many days your money will last, (as well as how much time you'll have) in order for you to truly be satisfied. Always remember, that additional expenses (i.e. side trips, unscheduled events, and 'wants', which suddenly becomes 'needs') must be planned for as well. So by allowing yourself, say...an additional 25% of your travel budget for these expenses, you will not find yourself short of cash,—and thus are able to enjoy your vacation time, without worry.

Over the past few years, my own experience has taught me that planning ahead also has an additional benefit: there is usually never a need to charge such your purchases at the standard 18% credit card rate. Bottom line: you are getting a great return on your money—18% SAVED vs. the palty 2% you'd earn in interest at the local credit union. (Do you now sense where the local banks really make their money?)

Ok, so now you have $'X' number of dollars with 'X' of days in which to travel and enjoy yourself. Your next move is to set the process in motion. So let's begin with the basics: Mode of Travel—Naturally, it is the airfare price that first comes to most people whenever a trip is planned. Yet here again, you should never pay full price for such a routine commodity.

I mean think about it—the airline industry offers hundreds of flights daily to numerous cities, yet their occupancy rates on many flights is often times less than 50%. Now since the plane is going there anyway, they obviously want to fill as many of those empty seats as possible—thus 'fare wars' (coupled with some restrictions, of course) are often times introduced. You role is simply to take advantage of these 'deals'. How? Well…you can try being flexible as to when you want to go. Also be open to various stopovers at other airports, especially if time is not a major consideration. And finally, consider arriving at a less traveled airport, that is still relatively close to your destination, and which also offers a low cost form of transportation into it. Now if you think this is not worth your time, then reconsider what your time is truly worth. For example, with just two hours of arrival time difference, I've saved anywhere from $400 to $1100. (Now I don't know about you, but personally, I've never had a job that paid me an hourly wage like that). One other 'bit' of information: one of the best ways to get a reasonable airfare, is to log onto the various airline carriers web-site. Since booking fares is done 'from computer to computer', it makes since that these 'Internet' fares would be lower—and often times they are! (Yet, published short-notice promotional airfares are usually even lower!) So always shop around for these 'hidden' deals for the travel industry is usually chock full of them.

Of course, taking a flight is merely one way to arrive at your destination. After all, this is where you'll want to give yourself lots of options. Just don't make the classic mistake of booking an airfare to your sole destination, without first thinking of some other possibilities. For example, suppose you have a $1000 and a month to visit the east coast. Here you have several choices. First you can fly there in just a few hours, get a hotel and then explore the area (via car rental) for several weeks. Thats fine if that's the only area your interested in seeing. If however, you'd like to tour another-or even several-parts of the US, you might want to consider taking Amtrak—the US train system. No, not all of their various routes are scenic and yes you might get restless after being on it for just a few days, yet the 'upside' is you can get off at various points (with specific travel packages), explore those cities, reboard (with reservations of course) and then continue on your way to your next destination of choice. So is train travel a possible 'cure' for the blandest of some routine plane trip? For some travelers it is. Clearly, it all depends on what your PRIORITIES (there's that 'golden' word again) are. Previously, I've done both and accordingly appreciated both for what they each offer—speed vs. scenery.

Still another alternative to consider is Greyhound—the nations bus system. I've also ridden this travel 'mode' both for day trips and as a weekly excursion venture. My own preference certainly favors the day trip—primarily because unlike a train, there is less space for you to get up and move around. Believe me, having to sit (and sometimes sleep) in the same bus seat over several days can certainly rattle ones nerves. Still, just a few hours travel to a short destination allows you the time to relax and enjoy the outside scenery, (which is something you would definitely miss from the air). Ironically, even in this day of jumbo jets, certain parts of the US still do not have close access to either the train or an airport, and thus the bus system is called upon to fill that need. So if your considering a trip via Greyhound, your best bet is clearly to plan an 'excursion' fare, where you'll likely receive the most 'mileage for your money.' Like Amtrak, the bus system also has its own slow season. Thus if you have the time (and desire) to visit some other cities, you might want to compare the various 'off-season' price packages of both. Just don't always assume that getting from one point to another is automatically best reached by air. Of course, anyone whose ever waited for hours in a luggage terminal for their baggage will know this from experience.

Still another source of lesser used travel can be found on the waterways of both inland and coastal America. For example, the next time your in the LA area, you might want to take a boat ride to the nearby (and outlaying) Channel Islands. By way of contrast, in San Francisco, you can take the ferry from there to Oakland—or from Fisherman's Wharf to the tourist 'mecca' of Alcatraz Island. A similar scenario applies if you should ever visit Burlington Vermont. There you can take a ferry ride to upstate New York via travel on scenic Lake Champlain. Take this trip in the fall foliage season and you'll likely get a true 'win-win' scenic bonus, as well. Other water 'routes' to consider—Seattle to Vancouver Island, scenic points along the Mississippi river, and even the outer islands of both Maine and North Carolina.

And should you ever develop a sincere interest for being 'home' on the water, you might even want to consider renting a houseboat for just a few weeks. Personally, I've never done this, but have since heard that it is really an enjoyable (and very different) experience. So who knows, you might even like the idea enough to permanently live in one, and that of course, would make such a vacation a true 'find'.

There is yet, one other 'mode' of travel which few 'seasoned' travelers ever consider—and that is the two wheel world of both the motorcycle and the bicycle. Granted most of the appeal for the former would come from those who who are well…physically fit, yet for someone who is look-ing for adventure in the wide opened spaces of western America, the idea of such a trip could make it all the more enticing for those folks looking to try something just a wee bit 'different'. In fact, bicycling has become such a popular sport, that today there are many organizations that offer biking tours to some very scenic locations, within the country. Now if your look-ing for a sense of adventure, there's one option you'll definitely want to consider.

In addition, bicycling offers a 'rush' to those looking for an alterna-tive to crowded cities, cramped hotels, and overpriced rental cars. Two methods of planning such a trip by foot power can be arrived at quite easily: either by your own planned excursion, or by your joining a biking organization which routinely puts together various group tours. Personally, I prefer the self-planned version for a number of reasons. First, you have no set schedule—you can ride 'x' miles one day, then take the next day to 'sight see' on foot. (In other words you are in control of your own itinerary.) Second, you alone get to choose where you'll spend the night. Maybe instead of a local motel, you'd prefer camping out under the stars—or maybe you'd like to share you road experience with like-minded travelers at a local bed and breakfast. Or what about staying at a local Y(MCA)? Third, and perhaps most important of all, you'll also substantially cut your overall trip costs by simply having a economical combination from both the 'eating light and eating right' rules of the road.

If your a veteran bicyclist, then you know what the guidelines are: eat a light, yet high energy breakfast (ie raisin bran, juice, toast) so that you don't get tired easily. Then for lunch, try a simple meal like pasta, which will also boost your energy—and thus keep you enjoying the ride towards the next destination on your schedule. Finally, when that much anticipated dinner hour arrives, you know thats also when the time to splurge arrives as well. So now that your ride is finish for the day, you can (if you so desire) eat a hardier(and fattier) meal, like meat and potatoes. Note also, that much of the previously suggested 'road food' can be purchased at local convenience stores (or diners) along the way, so your choice of what to buy comes down to your own personal preference. Now clearly, both food and lodging will be your prime expenses, while on your biking adventure. You can certainly cut both by simply planning in advance. Bonus Bit: Be sure to also bring along either a phone calling card or cell phone—in the event you need to call for road assistance somewhere along the way. For many travelers, bicycling is truly a fun adventure but obviously you need to be in top physical shape—and most importantly, to know your own endurance level as well. Still, if your serious about such trip, you might want to start by contacting both a local cycling club as well as the local bike shop, so as to get familiar with both the gear and trip guidance they can offer you. Now once you decide on your first road 'trip', you'd also be wise to stick to a short distance ride, primarily because you will certainly want to make some 'point of interest stops' along the way.

Bottom line—always pace yourself as to you own physical ability, and always try to ride for time—rather than distance.

Now in regards to the topic of touring via motorcycle, I simply say this: If you've never ridden a motorcycle before (or even routinely), you'll definitely want to learn its unique handling operational characteristics, well ahead of any planned excursion. Realize also that motorcycles can (and do) become tiring to someone unfamiliar with long stretches of desolated highways (ie Hgw. 50 in Nevada, also known as the loneliest road in America) that many times seem to go on forever. Still, if you pace yourself, rest frequently, and appreciate all the sights along the way, cycling is really an inexpensive way to see the country. Of course, for many reasons (companionship, shared expenses, and help along the way), it is usually wise to tour via motorcycle with another person.

As in the case of a planned bicycle excursion—our best bet for getting the right cycle for such a trip should come from a visit to the local motorcycle dealer. Here you'll get valuable 'inside' information as to the best equipment, the ideal season to travel, as well as the best places to visit on your trip. Of course, some of the talk will likely be bias based, yet it will also give you some further insight into the adventure that awaits you once you decide to put such a trip together. Now if your still want additional info, visit another cycle shop and/or make contact with your peers who also have a similar interest in touring. Either way, such two-wheel travel adventures offers a refreshing change for those who are simply bold enough to pursue it.

Lodging is without a doubt, a major expense component of any travel venture. Since there are so many alternatives to choose from (ie from camping to a staying at a five-star hotel), it is very important that you choose wisely when making such arrangements. Accordingly, each of the following alternatives are listed from the least to the most expensive.

Camping has come a long way—comfort wise—from the harsh realities of yesteryear. As a result, you can forget about being caught unprepared in the misery of a cold downpour, since todays campers can now retreat to the warmth and comfort of a RV (recreational vehicle) while also enjoying a home cooked meal from the RV's built-in microwave oven.

Yet even if your without a RV and can only afford a tent, such 'creature comforts' as an 'safety-approved' indoor heater and an AC/DC TV, will most likely make you more satisfied with the camping experience than your own predecessors might have been. Among the reasons: first is the construction of the dome tent, which over the past few years, has vastly improved. As a result many of these (ie 'Pop-Ups') can now be set up in just under a few minutes. Accordingly, if you have a family, there are some tents with zippered 'walls', in order to provide a somewhat, yet limited sense of both security and privacy. So what you want to consider when buying a tent, is as follows: A sturdy material (i.e. either canvas or 'rip-stop' nylon), which also has tight stitching—in order to prevent the unraveling (and weakening) of the tents joints. A rainfly—so as to prevent both cold air and rain from entering the enclosure. Simplicity—An absolute necessity for putting up and taking down the tent in just a few minutes time.

Although, you can easily spend a lot of money for a tent, clearly you shouldn't. Rather, look for a tent that has both a long warranty and is like-wise well-made of quality construction. Currently, that combination translates into a price range of about $150—$300 dollars. Yet when you add it all up, (and consider what just a tent alone,will save you over alternative lodging costs), you just might consider its 'expense', to be a true 'investment' instead. Clearly then, having a good quality tent is 'basic' to making your camping experience, an enjoyable one. So pack the right gear, take a deep breath, and appreciate all the beauty that awaits you in the great outdoors.

Now here's one other concern you need to know about if you are a camper and that is, the declining areas which are allotted to tent camping in both the county and state park system. It's sad but true, but more and more of that open space is now being allotted to RV's, so its more than likely that you'll need to locate a campsite in a rural area, of the area that your considering. Accordingly, camping fees also have risen to about $20 a night. In fact, in some areas, you might even find some independent motels that are willing to rent you a room for not much more than that fee. (Certainly that's always something to consider if it should be raining on your scheduled night of arrival at the campsite.) In addition, camping reservations also require an additional 'reservation fee', which can often times add 50% (or more) to the cost of sleeping out in the great outdoors. However you can cut those costs by staying at the less popular locations, purchasing the right equipment, and planning your excursion during the 'shoulder' season (ie late May thru June or after Labor Day). If thats not possible, then camp at some lesser known 'wilderness' area where the crowds have not yet discovered. Not only will you get more choice of a site location, it will also quite likely, cost you much less, as well.

Of course, just as important as a tent, is the sleeping bag. True, many of these are suited for below zero weather, yet they also come in all price ranges—and sizes. The important rule to adhere to when buying this item however, is to not buy a warmer bag than you'll most likely need—(read: 40 degree temperature rating). Thus, your best buy will come from buying a 3-4 pound fiberfill polyester bag, with an inside cotton lining and an outside 'rip-stop' nylon exterior. In addition, the bags outer stitching should have a 'diamond-like' pattern, so as to prevent the fiberfill from shifting—and thus creating so-called 'cold-spots' when you move about. So if your considering a mid-summertime camp out, don't buy a zero temperature bag. Rather look for one that's label for a warmer climate. In so doing, you'll save some super bucks. Money which then can be spent on other things—(or simply invested, for an even greater return.)

A step up from camping out is the budget motel. The word 'budget' however seems like a misnomer today, in that most of these rooms now rent for $60 (or more) per night. The initial 'budget' price attraction and lodging price 'edge' that these motels once had, has since been reduced by far better motels (and even many hotels, some of which are routinely located in major cities), and which now offer amenities like nighttime entertainment (i.e. a piano bar or a live band), exercise rooms, and often times even a complimentary full-cost breakfast. Ok…you might not want any of these so-called 'extras', but if you do, think about them, as merely 'low-cost frills'. Since a standard cost breakfast for two would likely cost about $20 at a nearby 'budget' motel restaurant anyway, if you then add in any additional cost for entertainment spent elsewhere, you'll soon discover that you can get a better value simply by going to the 'higher' priced lodging instead. However, its worth noting , that one important attraction of the budget motel, is that most of them are located along the main roadways—which makes for easy access, and especially when your tired after having driven all day. You'll also likely to find a national chain restaurant close by, so at least, time (if not money) will be saved. And don't forget that swimming pool, you know the one which always seems to serve as a daycare center for the kids. So depending on your wants and needs, your money can give you exactly what you desire, when it comes to deciding between a budget motel or one thats priced somewhat higher, yet offers the better value. The bottom line: You simply need to decide whats more important to your family—time or money.

Hotels are perhaps the undiscovered bargain of the lodging industry. No, I'm not taking about the $200 a night tab (plus tax) but rather, the discounted rooms that appear at various times of the year, with prices that range from $69 to $109. (Bonus 'Bit': Always be sure that the price given is per room, rather than per person—which can easily double (or triple) your lodging costs.)

Now depending on the area, you'll most likely find such super-deals on most weekends in urban sites (such as Boston or NY), and when there is little competition for the business traveler, as compared to most week nights. Since hotel rooms are known as a 'perishable' product (ie 'rent it or lose it'), many hotels have since discovered that 'half a loaf' is better than none. Now add in any additional discounts you might have (such as frequent renter offers/and or coupons) and you'll likely come out better than you might normally expect to—even while staying among the nations major hotel leaders.

Of course, when making your reservations, always add in the cost of taxes. Ironically, most people don't and are surprised to discover that their low rate is now 20% (or more) higher, than what they believe was their own 'guaranteed' rate. Needless to say, for some deceptive (and obvious) reason, politicians long ago discovered that its easier to get tax revenue from visitors than from the voters—who would most likely hold them accountable for such exorbitant fees if they themselves had to pay them. The problem with that premise, is that the voters do in fact pay, each and every time they travel and stay at any hotel or motel. The only difference, of course is in the rate—with some locations adding just 3-4%, while others set at 20% 'plus'.

You can now see why you always need to find as many travel related discounts and deals as possible. Think about this—if you spend ten nights in a city hotel at $200 (with 15% tax) per night, it will have cost you $2300. If however you can cut that rate in half merely by going at an off-peak time (ie off season) and then adding in any additional discounts you might have, you'll likely save 75% over what others will have paid. I don't know about you…but for me, that's certainly not too bad for just a little advanced planning on my part!

Now when it comes to hotel food, I have to admit that I'm simply a true believer, in such underrated fare. Quite simply, in most cases, the food (in my opinion) is good and not normally overpriced for what you get. And no, I'm not going to even try and justify that $9 bottle of 'no-name' wine, but rather just the daily food specials coupled with that evenings entertainment—both of which I consider to be very good deals overall. Sure the quality of both will likely vary with the hotel management, but competition has a way of giving all of us, an alternative in todays marketplace. Certainly hotels are no different. In fact they have even more to lose by not being quality competitive, since their 'food product' business is certainly valued in dollars rather than in dimes. Still there are some basic money 'traps' that you should be aware of in many hotels—among these are : The Gift Shop—Here you'll often pay a premium on many items ranging from a picture postcard to various 'over-the-counter' items. (Your clearly better off to buy such items outside the hotel where additional price competition exists.)

Valet Parking—Instead of opting for this exclusive 'service', park your own car yourself and save on both the fee and the tips associated with this elitist-style 'option'. Taxi's—Are basically another pricey mode of transportation, which are usually also waiting close by, in order to whisk you off to your chosen (and costly) fare destination. So instead of automatically taking a taxi, simply because its convenient, ask at the hotel lobby about any public transportation or private shuttles that might also be available. The savings 'pocketed' would most likely be substantial.

Now heres a real budget buster: Top Shelf (ie name brand) liquors served in the hotel bar. Yet, here you have three alternatives to cut your cost. First, you can bring your own liquor to your room and thus have your cocktail before dinner, (ie right then and there). (Your savings—think 300%—or more!) Second, you can always walk outside the hotel lobby and check the nearby restaurant window menus for a competitors price and Third, even if you decide to try the hotel bar, you might want to try the 'generic' (and often lower-priced) brand liquor instead. Since chances are if you order a mixed drink, you won't notice the taste difference anyway. Bottom line: you can save some 'big bucks' just in this area alone—if you simply take advantage of the present situation.

Bell Hop—Now, I'm not saying don't tip them, but rather just don't 'employ' them if you only have one bag to move (a benefit of 'traveling light'). Sure the privilege of having someone carrying your lone bag might seem valuable to you, but the cost of it might not. (Also don't forget, that a bellhop relies on tips for the bulk of his salary.) Bonus Bit: If you have a heavy bag, there's a economical alternative simply buy one with a built-in handle, which makes it easy to pull—and of course, 'tip' free.

Newspaper—Why buy one even for 50 cents, when you can get it for free? Where…you might ask? Why right there…in the hotel lobby!. Of course, many newspapers are routinely provided by the hotels themselves, while others are left behind by people who first bought, read it, and now have no further use for them. Aside from saving another tree, you'll also be saving another kind of paper, namely your own greenback dollar.

Laundry services—Forget it…rather do your own washing and drying instead—since most hotels have both a coin-operated washer and dryer. By using them, you'll definitely pocket the savings difference. In addition, if wrinkles in your clothes need to be addressed, most hotels also have both a steam iron along with an ironing board. Once again, its a case of time vs. money. I'm simply pointing out the alternatives.

Premium room movies—that will cost you several dollars to see. Since most hotels today have numerous free movie cables (like HBO & TMC), ask yourself why you would then spend $7-$10 for a recent movie when you can see it on video at home for $2 or less? Sure it's convenient, but so is your vacation time. Instead save the ten bucks and visit a nearby museum or art gallery. Movies can be rented anytime.

Room Service-You've got to be kidding right? I mean if you've forgotten an item from home, do you really want to spend $5 (or more) on hotel staff assistance for something as inexpensive as a comb or perhaps a bottle of aspirin? No way, instead get yourself up, go down to the lobby and buy it directly. Not only will you likely pay less for the item, but you'll also save on the tip you otherwise would have paid for the 'room service'. (An even cheaper alternative is to simply buy the item at a nearby store!) Bottom line: staying at a hotel can be a worthwhile experience, (and a real value as well),if you stay alert of both the pitfalls and opportunities while there. Clearly, if you stick with the basics, namely hotel food (and lodging) and avoid the expensive 'frills' (as previously mentioned), you can turn an upscale hotel room into your own 'Best Buy'. So sleep tight knowing that you've just saved an additional 50%—or more!

Bed & Breakfast Lodgings—For centuries they have existed in Europe, yet in America they are a relatively new (and discovered) industry. By its very name, such lodging is defined as well….self-explanatory. However, there seems to be one major truth about them that most inexperienced travelers fail to understand—and that is their own high prices. For contrary to most European B&B's, the domestic version is not cheap. A case in point: It is not unusual to spend $250 (or more) a night at a B&B that often times might be located in even the most rural part of a state. You might be asking yourself—then how are they able to get away with charging such high prices? The answer—simply because of the demand as well as the 'mystique' most folks have of such B&B's as quaint quarters in a passive, yet scenic country setting. In fact, for many vacationers, that same 'lure' seems to be working its magic quite nicely, as judged from the B&B's increased popularity.

Typically, upon entering a B&B lodging, your most likely hear some classical music playing over the main rooms sound system. (A sense of 'coming home' you might say). Now, if you arrive in late afternoon, you might even being treated to a 'happy hour', which usually consists of wine and cheese spread/or dips coupled with various crackers or chips. In the nearby parlor area your likely to find various magazines (unfortunately many of these are often outdated by several months) comfortable couches, possible a piano, and usually a scenic outside view of the surrounding area. Of course, your room will likely have the 'basics'—but little else. In addition, you'll often times have to share the same shower and bathroom facilities, (which is usually located down the hall) among the other guests. (An inconvenience if ever there was one.)

The beds however are likely to be very comfortable with down-filled pillows, extra soft mattress pads and heavy wool blankets provided as well. Breakfast will vary from day to day, but generally it will be nutritious and flavorful, with many of the jams (which often times come from their own backyard) and assorted baked goods, that are also made from 'scratch'. Be aware however, that breakfast is often times served within a small time-frame—usually 8—9:30 am, so if you need to leave early or want to sleep late, you might not be able to benefit from something which you've already paid some 'big-bucks' for.

Bed & Breakfasts do in fact offer a aura of uniqueness, but its price seems high for what you sometimes end up getting. For example, you could stay at a fancy hotel for two discounted nights, instead of one at the B&B for close to the same price. You'll also have more variety when it comes to food, since a hotel restaurant is likely to have more than just a few items to serve its guests. Finally, there is the 'discount' factor which many hotels use to fill otherwise empty rooms, which B&B's don't very often seem to have—or are quite unwilling to promote. Their bottom line thinking, is that since there seems to be a captive market willing to pay the high prices, why then offer a discount? Sound reasoning perhaps, except for one thing—during the slow 'off season' most people aren't usually aware of any discounts being offered at the B&B, so that room goes empty,—while the hotel room gets booked.

Certainly, its quite true—that most lodging options can easily cost much more than the highest priced airfare, yet very few travelers seem to give it as much price consideration (as airfares) when initially planning their trips. Yet, by carefully watching for sales promotions, and being flexible with your time schedule, you can easily shave 30% or more off your lodging costs. Of course, don't expect the facility to tell you about such savings at the time of your arrival. By then, you've already decided to stay—and in most cases on whatever terms (and prices) they offer. Accordingly, time spent planning in this area, will indeed, be time well spent! Car Rentals—(And other Alternatives for Getting Around)

We've all heard about the 'Big 3' auto rental firms—(Hertz, Avis, & Budget) and the numerous horror stories (ie those infamous tacked on extra charges, which can easily inflate your initial cost) that one encounters at the check-in counters of most airport locations. Yet, too many travelers fail to consider alternative modes of transportation when visiting a new city, whether it be in America-or even abroad.

Just as in the case of 'mode of travel and lodging', car rental is an area where some 'big bucks' can also be saved. But before getting into the fine points of the many car rental games, you might want to consider if you even NEED (there's THAT money-saving watchword again) such an expense for your visit to be enjoyable. For instance, in several large cities, a car rental can not only become a big expense,—but often times an unnecessary one as well.

So what then are some of the alternatives? Well actually there are several to choose from. Let's first begin with the most cost-effective alternative—namely, public transportation. In cities such as New York, Boston, or Washington you'll find it easy to get around by using the numerous buses and subway system which are available there. (For example, in the case of Boston, you can take a shuttle bus from Logan Airport to the Airport MBTA train station and arrive in downtown, in a matter of minutes. The cost—under $3). Remember also, that since the best way to explore these cities is via walking, your costs are accordingly, even less. (Several cities will even arrange a walking tour with a local guide, who will then inform the group about the various 'points of interest' you'll encounter along the way.) In many cities you can in fact, go from one end of the town to the other via several transit lines which also interconnect the many tourist site locations.

In addition, these cities offer discount passes—such as a 'day pass', which allows you to save even more, rather than paying individually for each individual trip. These passes typically combine buses with trolleys and elevator trains, thus allowing a greater transit system, in which to get around and see the city—along with its historical sites.

So OK, that might be all well and good in some densely urban areas, but what if you need to go where the transit system doesn't go? Well…here again, you have several options. First, always consider a taxi. Sure the cost per mile might seem high when compared to the bus and train, but it will usually be much lower when compared to the daily rate of a car rental. An additional cost consideration of the latter, is the parking fee which may be required at your destination. (Be sure to also consider that, if you do decide to go the car rental route.)

Another alternative is a 'shuttle service'. In some areas, you can share the ride with strangers and pay only your share—rather than the full100%. Recommendation: always consider this service before you consider a car rental. After all, the expense (and aggravation) of driving in a strange city (especially at night) can make one's trip more of a chore—rather than one of celebration.

Of course, if the distance is not to far away, also consider a bike rental. For just a few dollars you can get from point A to point B in less time, than if you were driving. This is especially true during the so-called 'daily rush-hour' commute. You will want to feel physically fit however, before you go with this alternative—especially in a city which tends to be very hilly (ie Seattle or San Francisco). Another consideration for you will be the type of bike which you can rent. Fortunately, the days of the one-speed bike are (thankfully) by and large 'passe'. By way of contrast, todays bike rentals can go from 10 to 21 speeds. Still you'd be wise to know before hand how to shift the gears and brake appropriately—(before you need to)—especially in dense city traffic. (Conversely, along some coastal cities, you can often rent a 'beach cruiser' and ride it with very little effort.) Bottom line: The best way to find out whats available in two-wheel transportation, is to simply look under 'Bicycle Rentals' in the Yellow Pages.

Yet, one other type of transportation alternative is the Moped. This might appeal to those who simply like the idea of the bicycle, but shy away from the 'huff and puff' image of climbing up hills. With the moped, the source of power lies in its small engine. The top speed of this 'vehicle' will likely be under 40 mph—but since most inner cites speed zones are usually less than that, this shouldn't present a problem.

As is the case with a bike rental, always be sure to wear a helmet. Accidents can and do frequently happen with both of these two-wheel vehicles, thus a helmet, in essence could save your life. Bonus 'Bit'—Nearly 80% of all head injuries are the result of the rider not wearing a helmet. So here again, you'll want to check under the appropriate phone book heading 'Moped Rentals' to compare prices before you decide on this option. Now if the distance is too far way, or if you need to get on a highway, your other alternative would be to rent a motorcycle. Of course, you would want (and need) to be an experienced rider, since most states have strict laws regarding such rentals, due to the higher speed capabilities of this two-wheeler. In fact, not too many urban areas have such rental outlets, so you'd be wise to line up a reservation long before you decide to rent one. As you can see, two wheels (or even two feet) can present a viable alternative to a car rental in many urban (and surrounding) areas. By using your own imagination-and employing advanced planning methods (ie 'reservations'), you can practically avoid the exorbitant cost that's so often associated with most car rentals today.

OK,…OK, so you still believe that a car rental is necessary for a variety of reasons—namely comfort, safety, and/or speed. So how then do you go about getting the most from a car-rental, for the least amount of money? In a word—'PLANNING'.

Certainly, one the the best places to start your search, is in the Travel section of the Sunday newspaper. There you'll find several promotional rates—some of which seem just too good to be true. Unfortunately, they are only partly correct, since additional costs like taxes and surcharges can often times result in a 40% (or higher) increase to that low advertised rate. Such detailed information of course, lies in the small print found in the bottom of the ad. Accordingly, this is also where you'll notice that a CDW (Collision Damage Waiver) charge—(sometimes up to $15 PER DAY), will be added to the promotional rate, UNLESS of course,you agree to decline it, and specifically do so in writing. In addition, the average rental sales tax is about 8%, yet,as incredible as that seems it's still only a small portion of an even much higher rental charge.

For example…a surcharge which often covers a 'daily title & registra-tion fee', is also applied to a whole variety of other charges—namely, a road tax, a contract fee, a vehicle license fee, and even a parking fee. These all come in the summary-like form of city and state surcharges. Now for those of you who feel that your not quite 'overtaxed' enough by now, then consider this: Yep, thats right, there's still one more tax to be included, in the car rental cost. It is simply known as the airport tax—and is often higher (usually around10%) than even the sales tax. As its name implies this tax pertains to car rentals which are located at an airport. Now, if you think you can avoid this tax by merely renting the car from an alternative location—then think again. This is due to something thats known as an "off-airport rate" which also results in an additional 5-10% rental charge. Thus, by adding in all the taxes and surcharges, you can expect to pay close to 50% more, than the 'promotional' rate that was advertised. Still if your feeling overwhelmed by all these 'extra charges,(as you should) then clearly you can fight back by primarily shopping around with the competition.

Heres how to do it: Always ask for an estimated TOTAL of the car rentals cost, including all taxes and surcharges. In so doing, you will have a level playing field for comparing rates from one rental company to the other. As always, be certain to also ask about any discounts that may apply to your situation, such as an auto club discount or being affiliated with an related company employer. Both of these discounts will benefit you in two ways—first, it will result in lower rental costs and second, it will serve as an 'associate allied' in the event that your dissatisfied with the car, and then need to file a complaint.

Once you have such information, you will then want to inquire as to the size and model of the car you want to rent. Know in advance, that many of the lowest-priced advertised rental rates normally apply only to a sub-compact car (ie Geo Metro), which most people find way too small (ie 'cramped') to ride in. Thus they often times end up paying more money for a bigger car. Of course,if you need the car for a week, you'll obviously get a much lower rate, as opposed to the routine (and higher) daily rate. (Accordingly, if you don't use the car everyday, you really won't save much with the weekly rate either.) Bottom line: even if you 'opt' for the daily rate, that's also ok, since public transit (or taxi) would likely cost you much less than an extra days rental rate would—provided of course, that either option would serve as an reasonable alternative.

Of course, most of todays compact size cars will have automatic transmission, air-conditioning, AM/FM/CD Stereo, Power Steering/Brakes, and other power accessories such as locks and windows. Yet if your concerned with todays high gas costs, then try to rent one with a small size engine. Sometimes the same car model will come in both a 4 or 6 cylinder version. Aside from the difference in horsepower, the 4 cylinder will normally give you better mileage. In addition, if you'll be doing mostly stop and go city driving, then a 4 cylinder may be just the car you need. And speaking of high gas costs, always be certain to read the car rental contract regarding both the mileage and refueling sections, to be sure that you have an 'unlimited mileage' agreement. Otherwise, you could end up paying extra if you have to pay an additional, .20 or more per mile added costs, for simply driving beyond the maximum 'limited' miles so allowed. In addition, replacement of the cars fuel cost will also result in a 100 to 200% price increase per gallon, should you fail to return the car with a less than full tank of gas. As you can see, renting a car is costly, which is why you should always consider alternative transportation (ie buses, trains, and taxi's), especially if you are staying in a large urban city, where many such travel options are widely available.

So to sum up our cost-effective travel plan is to: (a) plan to travel during the 'shoulder season'. (b) reserve a low-cost 'advanced' promotional fare (whether it be airfare, train, or bus), (c) use discounts and special offers (ie 2 for 1 rates) for food and lodging, and (d) finally try and use public transit-(or taxis), so as to get around in your city of destination. Clearly, if you are able to incorporate each of these 'bonanza bits' in your travel plans, you can have both a low-cost and truly enjoyable vacation. So never let the fear of high prices deter you from taking a journey to someplace you always wanted to go. Planning in advance is the key towards making it happen. So relax…and then go for it!

Chapter 5

▼

INVESTING TIME & MONEY
/(Contrarian Style)

When the word 'investing' comes up, the first image most folks tend to have is that a certain percentage of our money once set aside will lead us onward (and upward) to a better quality of life. So whether its a bigger house, a finer car, or a much deserved tropical vacation, the very lure of the word 'Investing', seems to resonate a highly positive image to us. And it does in fact provide us with all those things. Yet there is an additional component of the investing mind set which will give many of us, even more satisfaction—and that is simply the investment of our time.

A simple truth: from birth till our death each of us has 'X' amount of time. How we choose to use that can determine many aspects of how we enjoy life. So let's take an simple example of just how time can be used as a worthwhile expenditure—(or as a worthless entity, that offers either very little (or nothing) in making such time truly enjoyable). As with the case of how we spend our money, so is it a matter of choice as to how we spend our time. Accordingly, every evening, each of us will likely sit in front of a TV set and watch a program, that includes numerous commercials which usually offers us little information on the product that is being promoted (ie selling the 'sizzle' rather than the steak). Yet, many of us consider these ads as simply the price we have to pay in order to get the 'free' programming. (Free that is, if it's received via an antenna, and not by some overpriced cable system).

Now once you consider that 25% of every hour is devoted to commercials, you need to realize that this is valuable time (make that, irreplaceable time), that is being wasted, in most cases. (Well, ok there are some informative and attention getting ads, but overall they're very few in number.) So if you watch an average of 40 hours of TV a week, thats equal to TEN (I repeat, TEN) full hours that is being spent on watching nothing else except....useless commercials. Now if that sounds like a big waste of time—it is.

An better way to watch these very same programs is to simply tape them on your VCR, and then play them back anytime at YOUR own convenience. So what then can you do with an extra 10 hours? The answer is plenty...if you simply set your mind to it.

Heres a list for starters:

Consider the possibility of starting a part-time business. Basically by reading about something you always wanted to do, you can now take the first step in turning your own dreams into a reality. Next follow-up your interest with a plan of action and who knows, you might be the next millionaire that started a grassroots business part-time from his own garage.

Learn to do things for yourself. Now I'm not saying everyone is capable of becoming or successfully achieving anything they want to be, yet most of us can do many tasks we currently pay others to do for us. For example, are you paying a plumber $70 an hour to unplug a sink. If so, then learn to do it yourself (via 'how to' books) and keep the money in your own pocket instead. The same deal goes for minor auto repairs (ie changing an air filter, replacing spark plugs, replacing a defective headlamp). In fact, you can apply this same principle to many services you now pay somebody else for, and by so doing, you will gain both the ability of self-reliance as well as keeping some 'new found' money,—which coincidentally, still belongs to you. But saving 'greenbacks' is not the only benefit you can receive by using your time wisely. You can also develop an additional interest, that eventually allows you to take up a new career—and all the benefits that might eventually come from it. You can also volunteer your 'free' time to help others or to a cause that you alone personally believe in. Finally, you can use it to simply 'daydream' about possible solutions to problems which you might just want to think about. Possibly even coming up with a new invention for something nobody else has even thought of-let alone patented.

Bottom line: finding extra time is easy, if you really start to think about it. Yet, aside from adjusting your TV habits, you can also consider these other tips: Always try to plan your daily activities in advance. Simply by scheduling your time, you allow yourself the luxury of enjoying life without much of the stress thats often associated with the unexpected (and sometimes frequent) 'last-minute' calamities. Sure, the gotcha 'time bandits' will sometimes arrive, and thus throw a monkey-wrench to your schedule, but over the long-run you'll become more aware of what is important—and what can be easily put on the bottom of the (time) pile.

Accordingly, when a 'major' need arises, try and downsize your other 'priorities' or assigned them to somebody else. The main point is to keep both balance and a clear perspective of priorities within your own life. You can also keep alert for opportunities that allow you to accomplish twice as much in the same (or even lesser) time period. For example, when driving to work, try listening to an audio book or taped seminar, both of which you will likely benefit from. As an even greater alternative to driving solo is the fact, that public transit will also free you from the stress of driving. Now couple that with the fact that since both portable CD and audio tape players are so reasonable priced today, you can still listen to your favorite 'best seller,—along with reading the daily newspaper! Clearly, thats what' I consider to be—a '3 for 1' best-buy!

Heres still another way to use your time wisely: intend of always going for coffee and donuts (or some other 'fat-laden' snack), try instead to do some exercise via walking outside in the fresh air. Not only will you save some money, you'll also feel better—and possibly (or should I say, hopefully) even lose some excess weight.

Say, do you want to spend less time waiting in line at lunch? That's easy, just bring your own lunch from home. In so doing, you'll likely eat better and save some valuable time as well. Somehow, I'm always amazed to see 'time-crunched' people in those long-lines at a 'fat'-food restaurant, since it first takes such precious time (and gas money) to drive there, sit in the car while the order is filled, and then have to 'frantically' drive back to 'enjoy' their so-called 'fast' food lunch. Simply by bringing your lunch from home, will eliminate ALL of that—so much, in fact, that you'll actually have time to even enjoy your lunch—with some added time to spare. An extra bonus of course: saving money.

Now that your workday is over—heres yet another way to save time. Rather than stopping at the local supermarket to buy just a few items, buy them instead at the higher—(yes, I did say higher) priced convenience store. Reason—you'll save valuable time there, since the checkout line is likely to be much shorter (and thereby quicker) due to its smaller size.

Are you looking for a way to avoid the traffic jams after work? Then try to work overtime. (Now there's a sure-fire way to save valuable time while earning that extra money, you've always been looking for.) Work however is only one component of how we use our valuable time. For example, how many times have you driven around town just to buy an item that was advertised, yet was not available once you got there? Next time, call the store ahead—to be certain that the item is currently in-stock. Then tell the clerk to put it aside, since you'll be right over to pick it up. (A wise idea, especially for any 'high-demand' item.) Also, the next time you need to fill up your car with gas, try to do it while your already out driving, rather than making a special trip simply to save just a few cents on a gallon. (You"ll also likely spend more money if you do the latter, since a cold engine normally uses more gas, than one that's already warm.)

Other tips: Have you ever wanted to make use of that wasted time, while your waiting for the laundry washing machine and dryer to finish? Then, bring along some reading material along and soon you'll be able to get thru that 1000 page novel before you know it. The point is, you can find extra free time, you never even knew you had, if you just stop, look and listen to what your current living habits are. Thus by being as selective with your own time—and money—you can begin your lifes journey towards a much richer and fulfilling experience.

Heres some other time savers you might want to consider:

—Shop whenever the crowds are elsewhere. You'll get less stress and also better service by doing so.

—Always call before going to a scheduled appointment and ask if theres a delay. This will save you from waiting needlessly.

—Take your vacation during 'off-season'—to avoid the crowds and enjoy your time just as you had planned.

—Delegate responsibilities to others. This will allow you to concentrate on fewer yet far more important tasks.

—Before you call long-distance, make a list of the points you want to discuss with the contact. This will save you both time and money.

—Use 'speciality' shops (such as 'oil changes' only) for auto services— in order to prevent some other 'odd job' from taking your own valuable time.

—Always have a book handy in your car, so that your can read it, (a)when your stuck in stopped traffic, (b) while your waiting at a long rail-road crossing and (c) whenever you see the opportunity to read, primarily as a result of being in a 'time-bandit' situation.

And finally, always stay alert as to how you might be able to accomplish something quicker, or eliminate duplication, or expand the functions of a single use product.

All of these will in essence, add extra hours to your life.

You merely need to seize upon the opportunity for doing so.

Money of course, is the main word of how many people still define success today. Sure, the old saying that 'money isn't everything' remains true, but so is the belief that its better to have more of it, than less. For money allows us the freedom to do what we want, buy what we desire, and also travel to places we've always wanted to go. Money is in effect both FREEDOM and POWER. Of course, each of us can earn it, invest it or spend it anyway we like. Still, the different 'mind set' between each of us is that some people will always be poor, (ie via escalating debt) no matter how much they have financially, while others will plant the same financial resources wisely (ie via investing) and thus reap a windfall that allows them the freedom to be their own boss.

Now you might ask yourself, how then does one become a 'have' rather than a financial 'have not'? Well, lets start with the basic assumption of 'waste not—want not'. That simply means don't waste your hard-earned money on worthless expenditures which offer little or no benefit to your own financial well-being. An example: buying something which you'll use infrequently, versus renting it instead. Take the cost difference and invest the money instead—then watch it quickly grow thru daily compounding.

And where then would you invest it? Well let's see what your current options are. Savings Banks are perhaps the worst of all institutions for increasing your own net worth. The reason is two-fold: First they pay among the lowest interest rates on your account—but even worst they charge among the highest fees for its services. Thus between these two 'double-whammys', they clearly win—while you lose. Bottom line: Look elsewhere.

Credit Unions are a step up—(that is, if you qualify for one). Yet even their dividend (interest) rate is quite small when compared to other investment returns that are available elsewhere. The 'plus' with credit unions however is also two-fold: first they usually pay a dividend, (while many banks don't), but even more noticeable is that they usually charge much less in fees—which is clearly far more rewarding than its small dividend rate, since a mere 2% difference in a home-loan fee, can be especially rewarding when taking out such a larger amount loan.

In addition, Credit Unions also allow the small saver access to saving money by requiring only a small amount to open an account—usually $50, while some banks often require twice that amount. And if you fall below that banks minimum amount, you'll also likely see a 'penalty fee' on your bank statement, as a result. Accordingly, the 'saver beware' advice with credit unions is to simply keep a low balance there, while putting the rest of your money into a higher earning institution. That way, you'll get both low cost services, while getting a higher interest rate elsewhere.

Bonds are certainly higher earning—yet also come with numerous strings attached. One of course, is its 'market value' which can (and does) fluctuate with the changing market conditions. For instance, a bond you buy for $1000 and pays an 8% interest rate over the next five years might sound like a good conservative investment (and it is, for those who can 'gamble' on both interest rates and inflation remaining low during that time.) But if interest rates (or even inflation) rises, (and you need to sell the bond) the market value for it can be drastically reduced,—which means that not only won't you likely get your $1000 principle back , but you'll also be getting less of a return (in this case 8% versus whatever higher rate current returns are paying.) Conversely, it should be noted that this risk scenario can also work the other way as well. For example, if interest rates and inflation both fall, then your bond becomes a much sought after instrument in the marketplace. In other words, it will likely sell at a 'premium', (since its interest rate will be higher than other newly-issued bonds) should you decide to sell it then. As I mentioned earlier, buying bonds IS a gamble—sometimes you win, sometimes not.

Money Market Mutual Funds are basically an uninsured way to get a higher return on a 'saving-like' (ie investment) account. Here your money will be merged with other investors to primarily invest in high-quality debt securities. Traditionally. such funds will usually pay twice what a credit union will pay in dividends, yet it lacks the insurance protection and also requires a higher opening deposit, (ie $1000) to begin with. However, if your still looking for a higher rate for your 'surplus' cash (and which is not deposited in the credit union), then taking a 'risk' with a money-market mutual fund can certainly be a reasonable way to go. Sure you could lose everything, if all the companies invested were to go 'belly-up', but over that entire industries history, few people have ever experienced such a loss. Still, this one fact remains: it is a 'gamble '—and thus the greater the risk—the greater the reward (2% vs. 5%)!

I also want to note,that there is yet another rate for which you need to be concerned about when buying Mutual Funds—specifically its 'expense ratio'. This is basically the cost to you for having the fund operate on your own (and the other investors) behalf. Normally this amount will range from three-quarters to one percent of the money you have invested with the fund. Although initially, this may not seem like a lot of money, it does add up to less money working for you. So always be sure to compare this rate—as well as the funds current dividend yield, from competing investing funds. In fact, over time, that 'little' difference alone will certainly startle you.

Next, we come to the one source of income generation, which more and more Americans have now decided to invest in—specifically, the stock market. Clearly, this is the area of personal finance which over the past decades has routinely offer one of the best rates of return on your money—(12% on average). Sure, it would of been nice to buy Microsoft at $5 a share, as it was back in 1986, but thats simply just one of the many 'like-stocks' that even today, can make someone—(make that anyone,) extremely rich over time. The key to such riches of course, is to correctly pick one (or even several) stocks, which look as though they might be ready to skyrocket in value on any one of the numerous stock exchanges.

So how then does one pick such a stock? Well, If you study the industrys outlook, along with a companys performance in both good and bad (read: 'bear') financial markets, and then find that the company has a solid record of paying dividends regardless of economical conditions, you are likely to have found a real 'contender' (as opposed to a 'pretender') in the high stakes game of stock investing. However, you would also be wise NOT to put too much money into stocks, since a highly profitable stock could immediately turn into a loser from any number of unforeseen circumstances (ie a loss of public confidence in the company—or the country, as was seen in 1973-74 during the first oil embargo.) Always remember also, that even so called 'blue-chip' companies like GM or IBM, have occasionally been shown to decline drastically in value—even despite what 'professional analysts' had optimistically predicted for such companies. Yet, make no mistake about it—investing in the stock market is, in fact high risk. But by limiting what you can afford to possibly lose, you should be able to pick stocks, based upon the expected growth of that companies product and of that industrys growth projection as a whole. Of course, finding such a stock with a below-average (ie under 10) P/E (price to earnings ratio), will also go a long-way towards buying a quality stock. Just remember to initially follow a stock with some worthless 'paper-trades', in order to see how the stock performs.

Then once your ready to take the 'real' plunge and actually buy those stocks, you'd be smart to make that trade over the Internet, rather than with the 'assistance' of a full-service broker. By so doing, you can drastically cut your commission costs by 50-70% in many cases. However, if this is your FIRST stock-purchase, you would be wise to go with a broker, since he should be able to provide you with some additional insight into a companies history—or more importantly, its likely price performance, (which is based in part, on its recent earning reports.)

Buying stocks over the Net is relatively easy—just remember that if you lose money, you have only yourself to blame. Of course, this also holds true, even if you decide to use a full-service broker. Bottom line: either way offers you no guarantee, that you'll pick a winner. Conversely, if you are looking to get a 'guarantee no-risk' rate of return (18-23%) on your money, the best way is to simply pay down your personal debt. In fact, this is a real benefit for anyone who is constantly under siege from escalating credit-card balances which somehow always seems to continue month after month. Think about it. Even under the best of circumstances, you can only expect 8% on average in interest/dividends, when compared to what you are paying every month to the credit-card companies. So rather than putting your 'extra' money into a 'safe' investment (ie bank or credit union) at 8% (long-term CD rate), you should be paying off your out-standing debt of 18% (or more),—with no financial risk whatsoever to you. However, you will still need to be sure that you still have the funds (ie liquidity) necessary, should an unexpected emergency arise (such as unem-ployment, hospital expenses, or even those sudden (and surprising) rental increases).

Accordingly, you'd be wise to set aside a three to six month expense account, so as to handle such situations. My suggestion: a no-load 'money-market mutual fund', which also has a very low (ie. under 1/2%) expense-ratio. In so doing, you'll have immediate access to your funds, while still earning above average returns with very little risk of the princi-ple. The other alternative is that if, you fail to plan correctly, you' might soon find yourself among those paying 18% interest rates, of which you've tried so hard to avoid in paying all along. So whenever you invest money, it should always be where you can get the highest rate of return possible, along with the most comfortable degree of risk, that you find acceptable. Often times that also means 'value-shopping', that is searching for so-called 'best buys', so that you dollars s-t-r-e-t-c-h as much as possible. And while its true that some of us have 'surplus' funds to invest, it is equally important that we also plan for improving our own financial future, primarily by educating ourselves in the personal finance arena of both buying and selling. Thus, by looking at the alternatives (and weighing the pros and cons of each investment) you can clearly balance the economical scales in your favor. Will power, along with a knowledge of financial basics is essentially all that's required. Since many consumers have already learned to shop wisely in most areas, investing wisely also, can mean the difference between having what you truly want vs. what you sincerely need. Between these two, lies your own definition of what your financial life should (or could) be.

So plan your financial future with simple foresight, as you too, can also become among those who the others envy, while at the same time, fulfilling all that you financially desire.

Chapter 6

▼

TRANSPORTATION TACTICS—
No Rest for the Weary?

Here's some basic facts regarding current car ownership: The average price of a new car today is $22,000, and will be kept by its initial owner for about 7 years. During those first three years of ownership, the cars value will have dropped by nearly 50%. So by the time the car is sold (some 4 years later), its worth will only be about 20% of its initial cost. Now add in the high finance charge on that $22,000 loan over 5 years and your true cost suddenly becomes $30,000—and change. By way of contrast, had you invested that same money at 20% a year (via stocks), you would have easily doubled your money, and still had a decent set of 'wheels', in which to impress the neighbors. How, you might ask is that possible? In one very basic word—'USED'. Simply by buying a car that is now 2-3 years old, means you've just saved 50% over the price of a new car. (It's actually even higher than 50%, if you'd invested that money 'wisely' during that time.) 'Oh sure', you might say—'except, your getting a used car complete with somebody else's problem and who needs that?' Good question, but one thats really irrelevant, considering the higher quality (and longevity) of many of the cars on the road today. 'Yeah, OK then….but how do you know whether or not THIS used car is in good shape?' Answer: a computer diagnosis by an independent mechanic is one of the best ways to determine that. But let's 'back up' (pun intended) a little further, and first consider what make/model car, it is that you want, as well as the vehicles own reliability history. That information (and much more) can often be found in the annual issue of Consumer Reports magazine, thats published in April. Quite possibly, this is your best source for finding a good used car, which was made within the last five years

Here's also an important note to consider when reading about the various makes/model your interested in-and that is, the 'cloning' of certain make cars which are nearly identical to a higher priced nameplate. For example, a Chevrolet Prizm and a Toyota Corolla are virtually the same car, minus a few minor differences. Yet, the price difference between the two can amount to several hundred dollars. Of course, there are also other factors, which you will want to consider other than the car's initial price— (for example, the rate of depreciation, the cost of both replacement parts and routine services, and even the cost of insurance premiums.) But lets say, you've gotten all this information together and are now set to buy that used car. Your next step then, is to consider the various sources selling such a car. First and foremost, you should consider attending an auction. Most people don't even think about this 'gold mine' source of used vehicles, but if you take the time and know what to look for, its possible to get a very good luxury car for less cost than an economy model. (Trust me…It's true…'been there, done that'!). Of course, you'll also want to check Sunday' s newspaper, if for no other reason than to see what 'ballpark' price is being charged for the car you'd like to buy. With that source, you'll likely find both a seller with a true auto 'gem' to be 'had', and also a 'lemon,' just waiting to be sold to the unknowing. Once again, the same basic rule of having a local mechanic check out the car before you buy it, also applies. Now considering the dollars thats involved for that service (usually about $50), it's actually a very small price to pay, in exchange for the confirmation that you now have (or don't have) a mechanically sound car. However, newspaper ads, represent only a small source of where to find the true car of your dreams. Here then, are some additional outlets for buying used cars:

Web sites—which of course offer numerous possibilities among private parties. And while such 'virtual reality' images of your 'dream car', is no substitute for actually 'kicking the tires', (ie physically inspecting the car, in person., it does in fact, give you an idea of whats available locally. Still another source, (in fact, make this the most common source for used cars)—is your local car dealer. From there, you'll know that the used car has been inspected, and that you'll also will likely get a short warranty (usually 30 days) along with the vehicle.

The price here is likely to be higher than some other sources (ie independent dealer, private party, or even an estate sale), but then again, so is the probability that the car will be in better shape. However, shopping around can give you important knowledge about both the sources available, as well as what the best price can and should be. The bottom line— by investing some of your own time to 'shop around', you can easily save several hundred dollars,…and that, by no means, is not small change.

OK, so now that you bought the car, it still lacks some of the features that you wanted, but were unfortunately, unable to find. For example, that much heralded 'quadro stereo' might in fact sound tinny—and in need of replacement…And maybe by now you've also noticed that the summer sun seems to 'cook' the cars vinyl interior, or perhaps the fancy seat covers are severely worn and in need of replacement, as well. If thats the case, then all of the above 'problems' can be remedied simply by going to the parts department of your local 'after market' auto parts store— where you'll likely save some big bucks over what the local car dealer might otherwise charge. Of course, in addition to saving some 'greenbacks', you'll also have more product choices over whats available. For instance, how often have you seen a car stereo with CD player advertised in the newspaper for less than $150 (some retail outlets even add 'free labor' installation) as compared to some 'dealer supplied price list', which often shows twice that amount? This same premise also holds true for many routine car services (ie oil changes, tune-ups, radiator flush,etc.) as well. So the next time your car needs accessories, parts or even an oil change, be sure to search among the ads for such, money-saving coupons. For example, some outlets will offer prices as low as $11.99 for an oil change (versus the usual charge of $30 or more from the auto dealer or even among those national service franchises.)

In essence, this is but one way to instantly make 100% return on your money. Still there are many other coupon offers,—most of which appear in your daily newspaper/and or junk mail. And speaking of saving money, here's one sure-fire way to 'max' out your investment in car services—and that is to simply 'do it yourself'. Yes, I know, todays cars are too compli-cated for the novice driver to even attempt to understand it, so why bother? Well, the fact is, there are still many minor services that can be performed on a car by even the most self-confessed 'all thumbs' person. All you need is the service manual for that car, which can also be bought for just a few dollars, at most auto parts stores. And even if you never happen to open the book yourself due to some sort of 'self-intimidation', you'll still want to have one, just in case your car breaks down, and the mechanic needs specific information to remedy the situation, for which he may not already have knowledge of. In fact, this has happened to me on more than one occasion, so I know from experience that having such a manual is a true investment in keeping both your car running, while still reducing its overall costs of operation.

Now when it comes to other car expenses, clearly gasoline will cost you the most money over time—even exceeding the cars purchase price and after all the associated repair costs are added up. Currently, unleaded gas is selling for $1.83 a gallon at many independent stations. Yet, the same gas selling at several of the major chains is .30 cents higher. The quality difference between the two gasolines? is virtually zilch…zero…nothing.

Now, if you think little about your cars fuel cost, then consider this: Today the average driver will log about15,000 miles a year. If he is wasting an extra .30 a gallon on gasoline, he is in fact, 'burning' money to the tune of several hundred 'wasted' dollars a year. (And to add insult to injury, if you are paying an extra .20 cents per gallon for the stations so-called 'full-service', then you clearly have money to burn.) So if you want to improve the quality of your own financial life by having more money to either invest or to spend on more important things, one way you can do this is to buy the lowest price/grade gasoline that will work in your car—(in most cases, that will be grade 87). Some 'muscle' cars do in fact require a higher grade of gas, but even that gas is available at a lower cost, so shop around—as always! Still looking for some other money-saving tips on your car?—If so, then consider these:

—Always keep at least a few quarts of motor oil in the trunk of the car, just in case of a breakdown, and in the likely event that your several miles away from a service station. Also be sure to buy a case of it, when you see it on sale. On average, it will cost you 50% less, than what the service station would likely charge you. That same rule applies to both bulbs and fuses—(better safe than sorry.)

—Tool kits can be bought for $10 or less, yet they will easily save you hundreds of dollars over the years, especially if you use it to fix the car yourself.

—An old/worn carpet, will come in handy if you ever need to get on your knees (or back) to check under the car for any leak or suspicious noises. Not only will it keep your clothes clean, it will also save much of that 'later' (and aggravating) pain to the knees.

—Calculators may not seem like a money-saving auto device, yet when it comes time to figure out a repair bill consisting of several charges (along with its tax rate), it's likely to be proven quite useful. Of course, it also comes in handy for figuring out your cars m.p.g. Yet for a mere $5 'investment', you can toss one in your car's glove compartment. Bottom line: Its truly, a 'must-have' for anyone traveling on vacation as well.

—A tire gauge is also one of the best investments, you'll ever make— assuming, that is, that YOU use it at least once a month to check the air pressure in your cars tires. Try never to rely on the service station air hose tire gauge, since most of those are usually inaccurate by several pounds, which often results in under (or over) inflation, and is the prime cause of excess tire wear. Since a good set of tires can cost $400 or more, a tire gauge will pay for itself immediately by insuring that the tires always have the correct air pressure—and hence, are less likely that a blowout will occur.

—$20 floor mats can be considered a 'best buy' for two reasons: First they not only protect your cars carpets from grease, stains, and rips, but they also come in handy if your cars wheel is in need of extra traction, as when stuck in mud or snow. (In which case, you would simply position the rubber mat behind the stuck tire.)

—Battery Cables will also save your the cost of an auto service road call, (providing of course, that you can get the required assistance from another motorist), in order to jump start your battery. You'll clearly appreciate a set of battery cables, especially if your car breaks down, many miles away from either a service garage and/or pay phone!

—A Hand Jack will also save your big bucks on road service, by allowing you to change a flat tire, when there is no one else around to help.

—Hand air pump—you know, the type used to pump up a bicycle tire. Well, this very same item, should be keep in your cars trunk—primarily, in order to inflate the spare tire to its correct pressure. Reason: If you ever find yourself stranded in a sparse area (and/or without a cell phone), this hand-pump will likely make the difference between getting to your destination much sooner—rather than later. They sell for about $15. So think of it as buying cheap 'road' insurance.

Finally, the best way to save both time and money on your car, is simply to keep it maintained with routine oil/air filter changes, scheduled spark plug replacement, and weekly inspection of the engines fluids and belts. Clearly, saving some serious money from car maintenance is easy, once you decide to donate just a few minutes a week, to your cars overall mechanical health. And it really doesn't matter if its a Rolls Royce or even a Rambler, money is money—no matter how it arrives! So always keep both your cars 'health' and your wallets 'wealth' in 'tune' with one another. In that way, the term 'happy motoring' will truly have merit.

Chapter 7

▼

Unusual Ways to Increase Cash Flow —forever

You've no doubt heard of the various sales pitches that come in the daily mail, that promises enticing offers to becoming rich simply by stuffing envelopes, or multi-level marketing schemes, and even entering some foreign sweepstakes. Sure, a few of these 'ploys' might work out for some of the many 'die-hards' who are simply willing to make the long-term commitment in either time or money, so as to make things better financially. Although many of the respondents never really 'strike it rich' as so many of these offers seem to imply, they do at least offer a chance for learning a possible second career. Yet for the rest of us, we are often confined to either a 9 to 5 workday or the "gutsy' decision to 'risk it all', by simply becoming one of the envied and self-employed 'pioneers'. Between these two positions however, lies a financial twilight zone, whereby the opportunity to make extra money will present itself, to those alert enough to discover the possibilities at hand.

It should also be noted here that I'm not talking about a large investment in either time or money—but rather the desire of many consumers to increase their own income through a sort of financial 'adventurism'. Specifically, these are opportunities that cost very little, yet can reap some big returns over time.

And so,let's first look at where most of the money is today—and that (not surprisingly), is with the federal government. Accordingly, here is where you'll find numerous government grants which are (by law) available to anyone meeting a particular grant's guidelines. Of course, you can find out about all the various grant programs by going to a bookstore and asking them for a book that details the various requirements for each category. The book will likely cost you $30 or so, but the financial rewards can often be ten times that amount should you qualify for one of the listed grant programs. So be sure to check it out—thoroughly! Now how often have you sorted through your daily mail and suddenly noticed a low interest 'teaser' rate from one of the major credit card companies, but then abruptly tossed it aside, believing that you already have one too many of those cards already?

Well, if you think about it, discarding many of these offers actually amounts to trashing 'found money',—because in addition to these low six month teaser rates, many of these offers also present incentives that can easily put an extra $50–$1000 or more 'found' money in your pocket.

For example, heres a recent day in which, I'd received the following offers:

For a initial low-interest six-month 'teaser' rate of 2.9%, this credit card company would send me a $50 savings bond—for free! I could easily terminate the deal at anytime, yet still got to keep the $50 bond. Still another company offered me an even lower interest rate (1%), and then sent me a quality hand-made quilt valued at $100—at no charge.

Then shortly after that, another company sent me a 1% credit card offer, (with a $29 annual fee however), but get this, it came with a 'free' booklet of discount coupons valued at $1000. (Not really a bad deal, considering I shop at the listed merchants anyway).

Of course, these are just a few of the offers that people tend to overlook (r should I say…ignore?) in their morning mail. Numerous other offers arrive almost daily: 2 for 1 coupons at a local restaurant; $10 off an auto oil change; some coupons for a free dental or health check up and lastly, a man's haircut (with coupon) for just $5. So the next time you go thru you seemingly 'worthless' mail, take a few minutes and check out the offers being presented to you. Chances are you'll find true opportunity to make some real money, simply from what most people look upon, as merely 'throwaway trash'—rather than throwaway 'cash'.

Now are you looking to make some extra quick cash? If so, then try selling what you no longer want or need. Immediately, the words 'flea market' should come to mind. For this is where you'll offer your items for sale to several thousands potential buyers—many of whom are (like you and me) looking for real value. As such, you'll want to be sure that your items are fairly priced, or otherwise you'll have wasted both your time and money.

Of course, you will also want to also sell an item that will make it profitable for you to pay the required fee for simply renting a stall at that swap meet location. In that way, your effort will have at least paid you, for being there.

First and foremost, you should always think about selling 'in-demand' items like small appliances, TV's and even stereo systems. These usually sell fast and can easily give you several hundred dollars if they are perceived as being in good condition and also are fairly priced.

Other items such as bicycles also sell well. So look over what highly profitable goods might be collecting dust (and usable space) in your cellar or garage and then sell them instead—while pocketing some much needed cash in the process!

Now heres a lifestyle scenario that just about anyone would find quite alluring: 'Do you want to make extra $$$, while setting your own hours as well?' If you answered yes, then perhaps you should start a part-time business in a field in which know yourself to be quite good at. Oh, don't worry, you won't have to give up your day job—or at least, not until you feel confident enough with that part-time business, so as to devote your own full-time effort towards achieving it. Now if you don't know what type of business or service to offer, you can read several small-business magazines for ideas, or develop and market any type of product (or service) which interest you.

It is important to note here, that you should be really interested in that business, not so much as to what the product is, but rather that you will totally enjoy doing it, since otherwise you could likely failed—just as millions of 'aspiring entrepreneurs' seem to do almost every day. Of course, you will also need to check on what permits or licenses, your city requires before you begin the operation of that business. Accordingly, you will also need to set up a 'cash reserve' fund for the core expenses, that are associated with the initial start-up cost of the business. However, you can likely eliminate 50% of those initial costs, if you first start a home-based business. In so doing, you will drastically cut your overhead expenses for such things as extra rent, extra utility costs, and even an extra phone line.

Once you have taken care of setting up such a 'cash reserve',you will want to plan an advertising campaign to promote the business, as well as what media source (radio, TV, or print) will be the most profitable for that enterprise. Remember also to always keep all receipts associated with the running of any business, since many of these costs can become itemized tax-deductible items, on your following years federal income tax return. So, if you've ever had a desire to start your own business, but haven't as yet, now is as good a time as any, in which to at least investigate the possibility.

However, if your still uncertain, then contact the Small Business Association. For there you'll likely find some much needed assistance, in order for you to take the first step towards creating your own financial independence, (via owning your own business). Just remember that once your business is underway, it may take a few additional years, in order to show a profit. Yet once you do, you will truly feel like a success—because, quite clearly…you will be. One other important point: don't ever let the lack of money prevent you from doing what you truly want to do in life. If you realistically plan your personal finances properly, you should never have to deny yourself that which is important to you. So go for it, much like the millionaires of yesteryear did.

Day tripping for dollars is a term used to describe any number of jobs that although are short-term in length, (a day up to several months) offer you the opportunity to pick up a few extra bucks as quickly as needed. Here then are just a few of these 'unusual' positions that perhaps you have not really considered:

Election Day Worker—Sure it's only a 10-12 hour job, but the task is easy and so is the money. You simply need to get your name on the County of Register Voters list, as that will allow you to be contacted, at the next time that they need election day workers. This job seems to work out best for college students and retirees, most of whom traditionally make up the current election-day work force.

Donating blood is also a quick way for acquiring money. You begin by contacting the local blood bank to find out how much money they'll pay you for your own 'life-saving' donation. Of course, once that donation is given, be sure to always follow the nurses advice for replenishing the 'lost' blood, otherwise you could likely end up in the hospital, due to your own blood shortage.

Freelancing is the term often used to describe one's own service—as being offered for hire. And so with todays rapid (and ever-changing) 'new economy', there no longer seems to be the job security, there once was. Yet, now more than ever, companies are subject to the constant 'boom and bust' cycles which now demands, that their operations stay lean and mean. One way to do this is by hiring only those people who are required when such work arises. Thus the demand for the freelancer, especially the 'professional' freelancer, continues to rise within the growth of the so-called 'new' economy. Still another form of freelance work is that of the 'temp' worker. You know the game—you register with several temporary employment agencies, hoping that at least one of them will soon call you with a job assignment. However, the caution flag waved here, is that you can never be sure if any of the agencies will, in fact call. So contrary to the advertisement, that says 'you tell us when you want to work, then let us do the rest', simply means that (depending on the competition and the demand for your services) you may or may not be called for an assignment. As such, your clearly better off in relying upon you own marketing talents, to the highest bidder(ie company) in todays marketplace. One way to go about that, is to professionally make up a one page flyer citing your services. And although, even this will not necessarily guarantee a cash flow, your chances of securing long-term employment is certainly much better, than had you solely relied on an employment agency alone.

Now for those of you, who like to live even further on the 'edge', there's also the opportunity to make some big bucks in the field of Day Trading. Basically, this is when you have a knack for recognizing undervalued stocks, buying them at depressed prices, and then turning right around and selling them for an immediate profit. Contrary to what many people (and investors) believe, this is not an easy way to make money. Yet, if you first try your initial luck by doing 'paper trades' only, then you could soon begin to feel confident in your own ability to be successful in this sideline 'career'. Needless to say, in order to maximize you profit potential, you would want to start by buying so called 'penny-stocks' which allow you to purchase several thousands shares, for just a few hundred dollars. If your stock doubles in a few months, you would then roll the profits over and repeat the same process, over and over again.

In time you could easily be making anywhere from 10% to 1000%, on your money—(and believe me, no bank or employer will ever beat that.) Just remember, that the odds are against you for coming up with consistent winners, so always be prepared for the so-called 'promising stocks', which for some unknown reason, will often times turn out to be well....a first-class 'loser'. Bottom line : 'investors beware'—is clearly the best advice I can offer you, should you decide to seek riches-the 'old-fashioned' way.

Now heres some additional ways to increase your cash flow:

—Hauling away debris—you'll need a small truck of course, but the money is good for getting rid of yard waste, concrete, and rubbish. Since most city dumps now charge a dumping fee, you'll always want to include that charge as your own 'overhead' cost, prior to giving the customer a price for the complete hauling job.

—Computer repair—if your know the inside and out of several computers, then why not let the public know about your 'expertise'? The same suggestion applies for those of you, who can teach setting up a computer system and/or instructing users about how to get 'on-line' and then how-to navigate the internets numerous gateways of cyberspace.

—Sell food and drink at public gatherings (via a food cart)—You'll most definitely need a license for this service since you will be dealing with the issue of public health. Yet, once you start your business, the profits you'll earn are truly unlimited. Of course, you'll want to cater your 'menu' to the seasons—(ie soda, hot dogs, and chips in the summer; hot cocoa, pretzels, and those all-American style burgers/sandwiches in the winter!) In addition, always try to go to where large groups of customers might be, at anyone time—since that's where your likely to do the most business. After awhile, you'll likely acquire an accurate sense of what hours of the day/night are the most beneficial for you to work at that job. Thus freeing up your time, which can then be invested into other business ventures, if you so choose. In fact you might simply take some time-off, perhaps as your own 'just' reward, for being so successful.

—Teaching a course (make that any course) that you know well enough, to instruct others on. You should think thoroughly about doing this, especially if, what you have to offer is something that is currently in high-demand. In so doing, you can easily name your own price. This can really be quite significant, especially if there is little or no other competition to seriously challenge you! Important point: If you do teach such a course in a private enterprise environment, chances are you won't need any type of teaching credential, (that is, other than the experience and knowledge required) while teaching a course in a public facility means you most definitely would.

—Walking Tours (Of Your City)—You might not realize it, but in just about every city, there is both a history and landmarks worth discovering for both yourself and those always curious 'out of town' visitors. So why then, not do a little research, and then put together a package tour thats complete with promotional flyers, which will prepare you for giving a guided walking tour of those sites? An important point: Just make sure, the area to be seen is convenient and not too far away from the city center, since most visitors like to stay close to where the crowds are—(ie downtown.)—Sell Art—wherever and whenever, you learn about some local 'Grand-Opening' or other civic celebration (ie summer music festivals) that bring lots of folks together. Such events always seem to attract the creative community, who traditionally like to purchased art from among the local 'arts and crafts' population. So whether you happen to be an artist or not, be sure you also get involved with this 'upscale' clientele base, primarily by selling some art that you, yourself might have already. In addition, if you are an artist, be sure to make this known to potential customers at such events, via some sort of sign board (ie an easel would be perfect), which simply states 'Original Artist present'.

—Stay alert—This is basically your own subconscious at work, yet the outcome of which can certainly bring you immense riches. Here I'm basically talking about, your own looking at every situation as being somewhat improved upon. Therefore every time you happen to see a problem, stop and think about what you could do to possible rectify it. For example: When the inventor Thomas Edison saw darkness, he set about to change it—and did—simply by first thinking about the problem and then proceeded to counter it, via his invention of the light bulb. In fact, if you trace the backgrounds of many of our other notable inventors, you will clearly see that they all shared one very common trait, which was—persistence. So adopt a similar frame of mind and who knows what you might develop just from your own unique talent.

—Play Guitar, piano (or even a tambourine)—and you'll soon be in demand practically year round. The simple reason: music is the worlds universal language and thus is always in demand from simple weddings to prestigious parades. Sure some types of music are more popular than the others, but by knowing how to play an instrument, you now have a freelance talent which can generate extra income for you—both in good and bad economic times. Want proof? During the years of the Great Depression, music was one of the few businesses that continued to advance in popularity. Perhaps it was due to the publics own identity to some of the songs lyrics (ie. 'Brother, can you spare me a Dime?'), or maybe because some of those other popular tunes simply made people feel good. Yet, whatever the reason, acquiring the ability to offer such an 'artistic' service to the public, literally means your future income can be unlimited. Needless to say, once you become well known, you'll also want to look into other promotional avenues like radio, TV and the local media. Who knows, with enough practice and the right breaks, you might even go all the way up the top 40.

Bottom line: If you put your thinking cap on, your sure to come up with your own way for making additional income.

Chapter 8

———————▼———————

Rip-Off Report: the 'flip-side' to your own 'best-buys'

Psychic 'Readings'—Anyone who's ever caught a late-night TV movie, knows that psychic reading services are among the most numerous of all 'night owl' commercials. Many of these promotions often use a toll-free 800 phone number, which leads the viewer to expect a free reading, simply by calling the listed number shown on the screen. In reality, what you'll likely get is a free one or two minute 'informercial', that will then ask for your name and address. After that two minutes of 'free time' has ended, the taped message will then ask you, if you'd like to get a live psychic reading while your own the phone. If you say YES, you are most likely setting yourself up for a big financial letdown. Here's why: Although the cost of the 'reading' is mentioned (usually $2–$3 a MINUTE or $120 to $180 per hour) on the tape, the caller can never be sure that the 'alleged psychic' is a true psychic—or if, he or she is even fairly accurate. Too often, it seems, these 'alleged' readers tend to give just basic and generic information, much like the (free) daily horoscope that's found in your local newspaper—and costs only fifty cents instead. In addition, many of these advertised 'psychics', will often times mentioned that they have help the police resolve so called 'unsolved mysteries'. Yet to what degree of assistance they actually gave, they seldom mention. Of course, what many of these the ads don't tell you, is even more important than what they do in fact, reveal! For instance—What is the psychic's 'proven' accuracy rate? Since any statistic can be altered to get the desired outcome, such information is rarely reliable as to its validity. How long has she been a professional reader? The very word 'professional' leaves much to ones imagination, since these services are seldom regulated by law. In addition, does one reading alone qualify the psychic to use the term professional, in the true sense of the word? Once again, that question alone invites some investigation by the client. What credentials (if any) does she hold, that qualifies her to advertise her services as such? None…is often the answer, since anyone can claim to be a psychic, even whether or not they actually are. What guarantee of accuracy (if any) does she offer? Here you'll really want to 'read between the lines'. Reason: Only time will tell if she is accurate, and by then she may have either gone out of business or most likely 'moved-on'. Is the psychic's mailing address listed as a PO Box number? If so, your chances of being ripped-off are greatly increased. Does the state where the psychic is located, require a professional license or even consumer protection regulation of such practices? If the answer is 'NO', to either question, then think twice before sending your hard-earned money off in the mail to some stranger that advertises her psychic services, as being, one of the 'worlds most famous' (and/or even 'celebrity endorsed'). Although many such readers will make a 100% accuracy claim, the reality is most never are, as the simple law of averages proves time and time again. Bottom line: Don't waste your precious dollars on such bogus ripoffs as psychic readings. However, if your still interested in the metaphysical field, you might want to purchase an astrology book instead, and then learn how to do your own astrological forecast. At just $20 (or so) a 'pop', that's clearly a cheaper way to 'see' into your own future,—and possibly 'transcend' yourself towards even better savings.

Credit Card Annual Fee—This can easily cost you $40-$100 just for the 'privilege' (or so says, the credit card companies) of having one in your wallet. At one time, (long ago…and far away) such card carrying consumers were expected to pay such a fee. Yet, that was when credit purchasers were fully tax-deductible—and also when there were higher financial standards (ie annual income) in place to qualify for these cards. Well, as the song says…'the times they are a changin'. And so they have. Today, if you check your daily junk mail, you'll most likely find several credit card 'pre-approved' offers, that offer some other incentives (ie low teaser rates, free balance transfers), along with…believe it or not…no annual fee. In other words, the competition for your business by the various credit card companies has gotten so intense, that many of them now waive the annual fee altogether. The reason behind their strategy is simple: they'll make a lot more money from your 'on-going' credit balance at 18%, than just the $40 annual fee, that was once charged. By deleting that annual fee, many folks will now apply for credit, who might not otherwise had applied. Sure these same consumers might have other credit cards, but this card-issuer perhaps offers an even lower-rate in addition to no annual fee. The end result—competition has benefited the consumer, via offering lower costs—and with more options from which to choose. So the next time your offered a credit card which carries an annual fee, be sure to trash it, unless of course, its benefits (ie like a free companion airfare ticket) exceed its solitary fee.

Another credit card 'rip-off' comes in the offer of the various 'secured card' offers, that costs you anywhere from $50 to $150, in order for you to be 'accepted' by the issuing card company. Basically, these offers are sent to people who have already been turned down for a credit card due to one of many financial reasons (ie unemployment, bankruptcy, or even a court judgment etc.), yet who would still like to have a credit card, primarily for its convenience, in todays nearly 'cashless' society. Yet there are also several low-cost enticing 'deals' (ie a $20 or less one-time fee) for such people, who are interested in purchasing a 'secured card'. The best of these, is when the offer comes with a 'refundable deposit' on your opening deposit funds,(ie the issuer will grant you a small credit limit similar to your deposit, but not allow you to withdraw that money, in order for your credit card balance to be established, within a certain time period, which is usually 1 year). Of course, soon after that 1 year time period ends , you'll most likely start to receive the more traditional credit card offers in the mail.

Another bonus to these offers: some of these same issuers even pay you interest on your deposit—providing of course, that you pay off your credit balance when its due. However, If you are in need of a low—or even 'no cost' credit card, you might want to apply with your local credit union instead. Not only are you likely to get a lower initial fee ($10), its other fees for consumer services will also be lower as well. The bottom line: When you get a costly (ie $50) offer to 'qualify' for a 'secured' credit-card, take the initiative by simply cutting that one offer into two halfs!

Public Schools—If you can't figure out by now, why so many high school 'graduates' have trouble reading and writing, just visit the local government school and you'll see exactly where all your tax dollars are being wasted.

Accordingly, todays curriculum seems to put an emphasis on students 'feeling good' about themselves, rather than on learning any of the necessary marketable skills required by todays competitive work place. Now think about this—How many times have you picked up the newspaper and read that once again American students finished near the bottom in test results for BOTH math and/or science? "Too often".... is the appropriate answer, most taxpayers would likely give. Yet, these very same people continue to vote for politicians who advocate more money for "education, education, education"(while in reality too few of these voters realize that very little of this taxpayer money ever reaches the classroom.) So where then does it go? Well, much of it is simply skimmed off to the bureaucrats who tend to put their own financial interest over that of the uninterested parents and their children. The solution to this taxpayer boondoggle is simple: competition… vouchers…and other such proposals, that will stop your tax-dollars from being wasted year in and year out by these faceless 'rip-off' bureaucrats.

Currently, some 40% of California's budget goes to 'education', yet our children are among the worst performers on school tests,—in fact, they often finish near the bottom in certain categories. For this poor 'performance', that state's taxpayer is 'taken' to the tune of nearly $5500 per student /per year. By contrast, other states (with a much lower per pupil cost) tend to finish near the top of the list in student performance. Bottom line: money is not the answer—competition is. So the next time you have the opportunity to vote for a school voucher initiative, you just might want to vote 'Yes' and give the government schools something to seriously think about—namely…competition. If you happen to live in a state that lacks the voter-initiative process, try and get one of your local representatives to propose such a bill. Here's another suggestion: consider running for the school board yourself, since after all…it's quite likely that its your own child's future that's at stake.

Work at Home Schemes—Ok. I know, your well aware of the 'stuff envelopes at home' rags to riches ads, which is still used constantly by such so-called 'boiler room' operators. But did you also know that this is just one of the many 'aspiring millionaire' ads, that arrive daily with the rest of your junk mail? If not, then here's a quick rundown on some of them:

—For a 'small' fee of just a few dollars, the sender tells you to pass his request for money along to 100 other people. The premise here, is that you too, will soon start to receive money from others, just as the sender has already done from you. The reality is, they seldom due.

—Still another request for money usually comes in the form of a 'mercy plea', (ie unless you send the few dollars we've requested, a child won't be able to either get an education, or come to America, or get adopted,…

etc.... etc.) Should you ever get such a letter, simply do yourself a favor by investigating the company—before you invest. Clearly, any legitimate organization soliciting funds for such causes should be both credible and well-known, by the public. By contrast, a money solicitation from an unknown individual or group is most likely to reek with fraud and/or scam-like 'artistry'. The message here is basic: the sender is obviously trying to take advantage of your presumed 'emotional' concerns—as well as your wallet's 'content' (read: money).

So how then, does that person/company know such information about you—and your 'emotional' push-button interests? Thats easy—since all he had to do was to purchase a mailing list from a company that you previously had recent sales activity with. For example, if you recently bought a animal from a pet store, you could likely expect to receive several letters requesting voluntary donations to stop domestic animal abuse. In fact, such 'after-market' money requests seem to happen quite frequently. So if you've ever wondered how you get mail from companies that you've never even had contact with, well…now you know.

Conversely, if you want to stop receiving such mail from a particular company, simply contact them and request that they delete your name from their database. Unfortunately, you will need to do that with every company affected, for unlike the 'blanket' solicitation situation, there is no related 'one for all' deletion' mailing list.

Become Your Own Boss—might sound like 'heaven on earth' to some people, but the reality here is that the product or service, which the company offers, is usually questionable in value,(ie the purchase of 1000 miniature Buddha statues), and thus is unlikely to amount to any profits, at all. Of course, many of these so-called promising 'offers' require that you also send in an up front 'non-refundable' fee, which accordingly will sometimes even come with a 'satisfaction guarantee'. Yet even that ploy usually turns out to be totally worthless, as well. This is especially true, it the companies address has either a PO Box# or even worse…a foreign address While there are certainly many 'legitimate' self-employment businesses, you need to do your homework, long before you decide to send money along to a complete stranger who might be located far away, yet is known only to have a postal address.

Some answers for these questions, you'd definitely would want to know: For example: 'how much income could I expect to make if a reasonable amount of time is applied to the business every week?', (this should also require a third source for verification). Unfortunately, that's something which is not always possible (or even credible), if your only contact is from the sending company. Another issue for concern: Who will pay for the shipping and handling charges for any material thats returned? Often times a 'full refund' will exclude such charges. If you need to return books for example, your shipping fees could be quite high. So whenever money up front is requested by the vendor, always think 'thrice' (not just twice), before responding. Clearly, its a matter of 'buyer beware', whether your doing business away from home—or within the comfort of your own 'castle'. Simply by taking some time to research the various mail-offers, you can likely find your own true 'diamond in the rough'.

Still another get-rich quick scheme is the one that shows a former 'dead end job' day worker, now sitting on his Rolls Royce, while offering to tell you how he became rich—'practically overnight.' In certain cases, this promoter wants you to either buy his book or take some correspondence course, which he claims will give you the same 'opportunity', that he had. Nice try...but the reality here is, you'll likely have to pay a premium for some very basic 'business' information—such as investing in either the commodity market or in some other highly speculative real estate deal. One such book I read, revealed that the best way to get rich quick was to simply buy a lottery ticket—everyday, on the longshot that overtime you might hit the winning number at least once. However, spending some $365 a year on such a longshot, isn't a very realistic way, for anyone who's hoping to becoming financially independent. Rather, investing in ones own educational advancement (via academic/vocational training) would in fact, pay much higher benefits—and with a much lower cost, as well. So let the 'phantom promisers' of these mailings waste their own money—instead of yours. If however, your really looking to become your own boss, then simply start a business of your own. It really doesn't matter too much, what occupation you choose, just so long as you enjoy working 'X' # of hours a day doing it. To help you decide, some low cost assistance is available via books purchased from your local bookstore. Such a true (and low-cost alternative) will most likely, even allow you to end up financial independent—and on your own terms as well!

Finally, heres yet another 'rip-off' your likely to encounter:

The opening line on the letter says this:

'Congratulations—You've just won a free trip to Europe'. Then you begin to wonder…'is it too good to be true?'. The answer…you bet it is. Simply by reading the 'small print' further, you'll find the various conditions thats required by you, in order to get that 'free trip'. Heres how the 'ploy' works: as an independent contractor your part of a multi-marketing (ie 'pyramid) scheme with several other people working under you. Once they sell enough of the product, you will get the required points thats required to qualify for that 'free trip'. Of course, even if you do meet that qualification, theres very likely some additional strings attached. For instance, you might have to stay at the companies designated hotel, rather than your own choice of hotel. What this means is that you'll likely end up paying something 'extra' for that so-called 'free trip' to Europe. Another catch to the offer: you might have to attend a company conference or sales seminar (at your 'vacation' site) thats geared towards that companies product or service. Thus, what you thought might be your own time…instead now belongs to somebody else. And oh yeah, before you even leave on that 'free' trip to Europe, you'll sometimes be expected to call a 800 phone # and comply with its lengthy one 'plus' hour questionnaire. Clearly with such time restrictions, one has to wonder if its a 'free' trip you've actually won or just extra working hours thats been cleverly disguised as your 'own personal getaway'. Read between the lines, and what you'll find is nothing more than a time-consuming shell game. My 'bit' of advice—'say thanks…but no thanks'.

Chapter 9

▼

Cutting Entertainment Expenses
—As painless (and as easy) as it gets

Entertainment Expenses—has got to be one of the most advantageous areas of the family budget where everyone can easily cut their expenses. After all, when money gets tight, its far easier to pass up that $9 movie ticket, than it would be to not pay your utility bill for the month. Yet many consumers today have now placed the category of entertainment expenses on the same level as the true necessities of life, like food and shelter. That's foolhardy to say the least. I mean come on...think about it. If you were to give up watching (and paying) for Cable TV, would your world collapse? Certainly not—(or at least it shouldn't!) Now to some, the self-denial of the 'tube' might mean 'cold turkey', yet that's as far as it would (or should) go. After all, before there was cable, there was the antenna (which allows for unlimited free TV) and before that, there was (and still is) the radio. Clearly then, you do not have to pay the usual $500 a year to satisfy your video entertainment urges.

Want to know how?, then consider this: Suppose for instance, that instead of paying for Cable, you only purchase a TV Antenna system. Immediately, you've just gained the same access to most of the local stations which are also carried by Cable. The difference of course, is that, the antenna delivers free programming, once the small ($5-$50) purchase cost for the antenna is deducted. Yeah…well ok, but what about the other channels that only Cable can provide? Well, here's certainly one alternative, which even most cable subscribers fail to consider: try renting those programs or movies at the local video store instead. True, you might have to wait three months or so, for it to become available on video, but that's not so bad, when you realize you no longer have a $40 month cable bill. Heres another 'bonus'—not only will you get to watch the 'cable' movie when you want to, but you'll also be paying for just what you'll actually view—rather than some 500 channels, of which you might normally watch only 4 or 5 channels—(the majority of which are broadcast stations anyway!

Bottom line: If you take that $500 instead, and invest it in your future, within just one year you'll have $550—$600 in your investment account, which will most likely give you far more enjoyment than most of those repeat cable TV shows (and recycled movies) ever will. Clearly, Cable TV does not deserve its place among the necessities of life. So the next time you send payment to the Cable operator, ask yourself this question—Am I really getting my moneys worth for this 'premium' cost service, since I'm already getting half of the total programming for free anyway? My suggestion : junk the service, buy yourself an antenna, then rent whatever movies you want. You'll get 90% of what Cable provides at only 10% of its cost.

Just as absurd as spending $500 a year on Cable TV is to spend $9 to see a first-run movie. Sure movies cost some $50 plus million dollars to make today, yet too often we leave the theater feeling as though we've been ripped-off, perhaps due to an uninteresting story line, or because that hyped 'blockbuster' of a movie simply had a popular 'star' in it, yet offered little else. Here's another point that certainly worth mentioning : try never to patronize movie studios (and their films) which routinely offer insulting and often times offensive movies. Remember, Hollywood can only survive at the box office. So if your wish to send them a message, don't pay the premium charges they require for showing a first-run movie. As an alternative, either wait three months for the movie to play at the local theater, (usually at a cost saving of 75%) or rent the video, which will be even cheaper still.

Now aside from the cost saving on the ticket price, you'll also save some big bucks, by simply not paying for the fat-laden 'artifical-flavored' popcorn (currently $4.50 a tub), or even that cold 'hot dog' thats so often served on a stale tasting bun @$3. Best of all, you get to watch the movie from your own easy chair rather than from some squeaking (and well-worn) tight-fitting seat.

Fuzzy math?…No way. Just consider this: If you attend a first run movie once a week, and then buy popcorn, a soda, and an hot dog, your spending $1000 a year. Think you can't find of a better way to invest that money? Then think again—about that next vacation, which you always wanted to take…or saving towards your own retirement, or perhaps even investing in some 'self-help' learning courses. Each of those is certainly where you'll get the best value for your money—rather than wasting both your time and money on something as shallow in substance as a make believe Hollywood movie. So stay home, pop your own microwave popcorn, and relax in the comfort of your own recliner, while watching a movie which others might have paid four times or more to see. In time, your investment account will thank you for it!

Live Concerts usually result in $50 seats, valet parking, and high concession prices at intermission. Throw in the various 'trinkets' and/or souvenirs and you can easily figure on $100 per person/per event. Heres a better way—try and see if the group you want to view, had their last concert videotaped. You can find that out by simply going to the video store and looking under the 'Concerts' category. If so, then here's a way to see the same performance for dimes rather than with dollars.

Accordingly, before renting the tape, always be sure to look at the time length of the concert listed on the label. If its at least one-hour long, then you know that this was the complete concert, since this is usually the amount of time a live performance is performed. Of course it won't be like 'being there', but if all you want is to see and hear the group perform, then you've just saved over 90% (or more) with this alternative. Now here's an added bonus to boot: You can watch the videotape anytime and as often as you like, for just a few dollars in rental fees. Bottom line: Seriously think about this 'financially-friendly' alternative when compared to those sky-high prices of a 'live' performance. If your still set however on attending the real thing, heres a few tips you can employ to cut your expenses:

First, always buy your ticket directly at the theater box-office. This will save you the usual $5 'plus' handling fee charge, thats mandated by the promotional companies like Ticket master. In addition, the chances are, you'll also get to pick which seats you want, rather than what seats your assigned to, by the ticket promoters. Heres another tip: always keep both your eyes and ears open for any notice of discount tickets, which might be advertised on either radio or TV. Although, this might amount to saving only $5—$10, be sure to take advantage of the offer, as it means more money is left in your pocket, rather than that of the promoters. Be sure to also check the price difference for a week night performance, versus a weekend show, since sometimes the former can be discounted as much as 15%. (Thus, once again, this saving becomes YOUR saving.) Also try not to patronize the over-priced concession stand, too often. As an alternative, treat yourself to a fine restaurant meal just prior to the concert. In most cases this can mean both 'food and drink' at a fraction of what you would have paid at the concert, for basic 'junk-food' (ie pepperoni pizza, hot dogs, and $6 beers).

Additional way's to cut those concert prices : Although many fans on the West Coast don't take advantage of it, in both Reno and Las Vegas, they can usually see a particular group for a mere fraction of what they would normally pay elsewhere. This is made possible, simply because the performances are used as an inexpensive lure, in order to get customers into those cities more profitable gambling environments. So if you happen to live close to either city, be sure check out what concerts are scheduled and then consider going there for some good old-fashion entertainment…and reasonable rates as well.

And speaking of concerts—if your looking for an alternative to pricey souvenirs, try the local music store instead. Here you'll often times find blown-up posters of many groups as well as trinkets (i.e. key chains, plastic statues, etc.) that are sometimes used to promote the groups CDs. Or you can simply think low-cost at the concert and buy just one or two items as a future memento to that evenings outing.

The important thing however, is to set a limit on how much you want to spend and then stick to it. Otherwise, that $100 concert could end up costing you easily three times as much—or even more. Of course, the choice is entirely yours, I've merely offer some viable alternatives.

And speaking of alternatives, lets not forget the exorbitant cost of $20 parking while at the concert. Instead of paying such high fees, you just might want to call the local transit company and see if they offer a charter bus to and from the concert. If so, your in luck—as you'll likely save both time and money. First, you'll pay just a few dollars rather than the $10-$20 thats usually charged for concert parking. Second, instead of being trapped in bumper to bumper traffic (both before and after the concert), you'll likely get home faster on the bus, since it will usually be given traffic 'priority' either by the traffic guard or simply because only the bus can use the express lane. So check into the possibility, since sometimes it works out to your benefit.

However, one time it might not work out, is when you have four or more people in the car. Since the parking charge is set per vehicle, rather than per person, even a $10 charge would seem reasonable, when compared to paying the alternative bus fare of $5 per person Now so far as the traffic goes, sometimes car pool lanes are also opened after the concert, simply in order to expedite the traffic flow as quickly as possible. If that is the case, then by all means you might want to consider car pooling instead.

Thus by shopping around for your concert tickets, looking for any discount coupons that might be available, shying away from the concession stand, keeping your souvenirs purchases to a reasonable amount, and by using public transit, you can easily trim your total concert cost by one-third or more. Lets see…thats $33 on a $100 evening out—not really a bad 'rate of return' for just a little foresight, hey?

Professionals sports also falls under the preceding advice, except here you have an even greater incentive in which to save some 'super bucks'. Your best alternative to those obscene ticket prices: simply watch the event on TV. Aside from the obvious cost savings, you can also simply turn-off the TV once it becomes apparent that the game is likely to be a certain 'blow-out'.

For example, how many "Super-Bowl" games in recent years have become exactly that—a 'blow-out' event? It would seem to be far too many—if you look at the statistics. Just be glad that you didn't add insult to financial injury by having spent several hundred dollars to 'experience' it 'in-person'. Yet, if you still want that 'in-crowd' atmosphere however, (and at a lower cost) then you can join that games other fans at the local sports bar, where believe it or not, it is sometimes less costly (thanks to the 'free' food and reduced drink specials) to watch the game there, than it would be at home. Not only that, but you'll also get to see the 'big game' on a larger screen. (I've even been to some locations, where the TV was the dimension of a medium size—theater screen). Bottom line: By adding in the food and drink specials, plus a minimum of traffic (as compared to the fifty thousand 'plus' stadium crowd), its clear that you've got one of the best entertainment values around today.

So ok, but not everybody is into the sports scene when it comes to interesting 'places to go' on the weekend.

So where then are the best places/events to go, in order to get the best value for your money? For starters, you might want to contact your local community for upcoming events. Here you'll find lots of information on live theater, popular concerts, and minor league sports, all of which are available for just a fraction of the cost, for what the 'pro's' would charge. Yeah…all right, but is the quality of such events the same? Truthfully—sometimes yes and sometimes no. Personally, I've never attended a live theater performance that has not been professionally conducted. In fact, some of these plays have been exceptionally well performed, in addition to the reasonable ticket prices, that were charged. Even the bare-bones concession prices were attractive…50 cents for coffee, $1 for a hot dog or box of popcorn! This same 'local' deal also applies to many 'family-friendly' concerts. No, you won't see the 'most popular' groups playing there, but you will likely find that evenings performance to be still very entertaining. And once again, at only a fraction of the 'name-brand' and often heavily promoted version.

Community Colleges—in particular, seem to offer a great value for the money, as well as an opportunity for looking into other upcoming events (ie arts & crafts fairs) while your there, (for the concert). In fact, several Broadway plays are routinely presented here, with ticket prices that cost less, than a first-run movie ticket would.

Now, in reference to most 'minor-league' sports: No, its not the World Series, but I've been to several minor-league baseball games where the teams score were truly 'neck and neck' throughout the night, even right up to the final pitch. Now that's certainly about as good as you can possibly hope for, so you just might want to try attending one of these games if you never have before. By the way, discount tickets for these games are often available in the sports section of your local paper—and usually in the form of a 'two-fer-one' to boot. Thus two general admission tickets should end up costing you just $10 for an entertaining three hours or so. (Personally,I consider that to be a 'best buy' if ever there was one). And finally, don't forget that many of todays professional sports 'stars', got their first start towards stardom by simply playing for such a team.

Some other local events that are either free or low-cost: Art Exhibits. It's true, here you'll get to see not only the local artists paintings, but also several visiting national art shows which might only last just a few weeks. Still, this gives you the opportunity to see some of the works from some of the major artists of our time.

The cost: usually only a few dollars at most. Often times, weekday admission is discounted even less. Your source for any coupons: the weekend entertainment section of your local newspaper.

Looking for an lower alternative to Disneyland, Great America, or Six Flags? If so, then consider a nearby roller-coaster theme park. Here you'll find a full days enjoyment with rides and events geared to all age groups. The cost—a mere fraction of the 'name-brand' alternative theme park. Although most of these lower priced parks are usually situated along the coast, they are occasionally situated within some larger city limits, in order to attract the largest number of customers possible. Of course, it's not only ticket prices that are lower there, so is the food, many individual rides and the majority of special events. An added benefit: You only buy tickets for the entertainment you want, rather than purchasing one higher-priced ticket for all. In addition—on many 'ticket slow' weekdays, the prices are reduced even further still. Or for true 'rock-bottom' pricing you can try attend after 5pm, when in many locations, discounted coupons are often times still accepted, as well.

Always remember that regardless of what entertainment event you are interested in attending, realize that there are low-priced tickets to many events, and which can be found in several outlets: among these are the back of local grocery receipts, inside the Entertainment Publication book, and yes…even in the Yellow Pages. Chances are also, that if the event is being promoted on either radio or TV, a discount coupon is usually available locally, as well. You simply need to take advantage of the opportunity—and 'pocket' the difference. Additional sources for savings: sometimes the coupons will come with your daily junk-mail, other times they might appear on the package of your morning breakfast cereal, but most likely they will be discovered where so few people seldom bother to look—inside their local newspaper—(usually in either the sports or entertainment sections).

Ironically, in recent years, both subscribers and readership has fallen drastically with the 'dailys'(newspapers), for any number of reasons. As a result, event promoters find the cost of print advertising to be quite reasonable (since lower print costs equates into higher profit margins) when compared to advertising on either radio or TV. Bottom line: a 'win-win' situation for both the company and the consumer. So keep an eye out for '2 for 1' tickets, related mail-in rebate offers, and special bonus deals. (In fact, you can think of such deals, as a 100% return on your money.) One more note: All such discounted events are usually 'heavily hyped' within some two weeks of the shows scheduled date, thus given you the 'early-bird' opportunity to get the best seats available—along with a reasonable cost.

Want to hear your favorite author discuss himself and his recent novel for free? Then contact the local bookstore and ask if they offer such personal events. If so, you'll likely be treated to a 'one on one' in-person experience, as the author clearly explains his background, along with the details as to how and why, he wrote that particular book. Often times, the author will then take questions from the audience, which will offer further insight into the author as well as his other published works. Most towns (with a population of 50,000 'plus'), routinely offer such events, and usually publish a 'Calendar of Events, of all upcoming seminars. So get yourself a copy of the book stores 'speakers schedule' and be prepared to be impressed for a time that is clearly well spent.

Now if your still looking for some additional free entertainment—then you might want to try attending an auction. After all, there are many types to consider including auto, art, estate and even some notable collectibles like stamps, and those always in-demand legendary baseball cards.

Of course, you'll initially want to attend that event merely as a spectator. Yet once you get the knack for both the quality and price of the items offered, you then might possibly want to bid on some of the articles yourself. Just don't make the common mistake of bidding at too high a price. In order to prevent that, you need to know what the item is worth prior to your bid being placed.

This can be accomplished, by attending the free inspection 'preview period', which is usually held on the day before the scheduled auction. At a recent event, shoppers have often picked up cars at bargain prices, original art at a fraction of its true cost, and several valuable estate items noted for their noted craftsmanship, yet were now selling for a 'dime on the dollar' basis. Of course, all sales are final. So if you misjudged either the price or the quality of the purchased item, your totally stuck with it—(ie buyer beware!) Bottom line: heres your real chance to obtain some super buys,(with most selling at a fraction of their original cost), and which also are just waiting to be had.

Thus, by knowing an items true worth and then bidding lower than that price, you too can likely become among the 'rich and famous'…(or at least among the auction set, that is.)

As you can see, there are several alternatives to expensive theme parks or exorbitant over-priced sporting events—yet even those alternative and high-priced events can be brought down even lower in price, simply from your own shopping awareness for promotions and/or discount coupons. Face it, just about anything that is sold today is also available at a discount. So with this in mind, try never to pay full-price for anything—ever again!

Eating Out—Cutting your Costs to the Billfold 'Bone'

Ok, so you've had a busy day and you don't feel like fixing a full-course dinner at home from scratch. Likewise, you also know that many (if not most) of the frozen food entrees taste like…well…cardboard, with an insulting premium price to boot ($5-$7 on average).

So what then can you do, in order to get good food at a reasonable price, with practically little or no effort on your part? Well heres one sug-

gestion: simply try one of the local restaurants for their so-called discounted 'early-bird' dinners (usually this is offered 4:30 to 6pm on weekdays.) Here you'll get the same dinner that's served at 6:01 (and later) but
with an added bonus—namely, a saving of 25% or more. You'll also likely
get better service then, since the restaurant won't normally be as crowded.
(Hey folks…We're talking' about a real 'two for one' deal here.)

Another alternative: You say you can't make the early-bird hour? Then
consider buying your 'ready' made dinner from the local supermarket
instead. Today most of these 'in-store' deli's offer a fresh choice of roasted
chicken, meatloaf, Virginia baked ham and even premium roast beef that
comes complete with two or more side orders for nearly the same price
you would likely pay for one of those premium, yet tasteless frozen 'dinner
entrees'. You can really believe it then, when I say that there's simply no
comparison—between the two (fresh vs. frozen). An added plus—you'll
actually get to see what your buying before you pay, rather than finding
out later that whats inside that enticing package is actually quite different
from what is shown on the outside carton.

In addition, today many of the 'supers' now have ethnic food (especially Chinese and Mexican) that is both freshly made and flavorful for
anyone wanting to taste some international fare. So check it out,as you'll
likely find some good deals—along with a reasonable price, as well.

Hmmm…still hungry ant not quite satisfied? Then check your local
paper for the so called 'all you can eat buffets' which usually includes several different entrees along with a beverage and dessert for one set price. If
your hungry, and don't want to spend much money, this is certainly one of
the ways to go. Just as good as a food buy, is a cafeteria-style restaurant
where the food is perhaps not as fancy as some other 'upscale' restaurant,
but where the 'grub' is often good (to very good)—and the prices are quite
reasonable to boot.

Of course, sometimes you just might want a meal thats made from
scratch? That's usually easy enough to do—if you plan ahead. Simply
make what you want for dinner the night before, refrigerate it, and then

pop it in the microwave—(basically,the same process you would do with a frozen entree) and presto, you've got 'home cooked' dinner made in just 5 minutes—or less.

There are other ways that the cost of eating out can always be reduced. Heres a list of simple ways to do it:

—Try visiting a restaurant thats located in a 'blue-collar' town. Chances are the lower-cost of living there will be reflective in the restaurants overall prices, as well.

—Try ethnic restaurants for both variety and reasonable prices. Most will offer a 'combination' plate, which allows you the chance to try several different foods, yet at a reasonable price.

—Seldom (if ever) order soft drinks or desserts, since both of these is where the restaurants highest profits come from. (ie a 25 cent soda from a vending machine will usually cost $2.50 there—a markup of 1000%). Much worst, is the 'premium' cost of hard-liquor drinks (as well as both beer and wine),—whether their ordered from the bar…or even at the dinner table. The solution: Make (and enjoy) your own drinks at home.

Now so far as dessert goes, you also just might want to wait until you get home before indulging in such 'extras'. For not only will you likely get a quality drink/dessert, you'll also give yourself a saving of roughly 1000%. In time, both your health and wealth will thank you for doing so.

Here's some additional food for thought, when dining out:

—Always call the restaurant thirty minutes or so before you leave home, so as to inquire if there will be any delay in your scheduled reservation. Often times some restaurants which also have cocktail bars, will tell you that once you've arrived, they'll likely be a 'short wait of ten minutes or so'. Be aware of this ploy, as this is when you can be expected to be shuffled off to the highly profitable cocktail bar for 'just one drink—(or two—or perhaps…maybe even three)'. Don't fall victim to this scam, as you can easily spend more on just two drinks, than the total cost of your entire meal. Now if you really want to save some serious money, here is a way you can beat the opposition at its own game. Simply arrive at your previously confirmed seating time—(ie no wait—no waste!) I've done this in the past and its work out perfectly. And although, the restaurant would still like to extract as much profit from you as possible (via selling your over-priced cocktails at the bar), on the other hand, they certainly don't want to lose their main restaurant business by keeping you waiting any longer than necessary,—since theres a strong possibility, that you might leave and then go to a nearby competitor instead. So feel free to play the 'just in time' waiting game—since the chances are, that nine times out of ten you'll win. And even in that one case when you don't, always be certain to complain about that 'unacceptable long-wait' to the manager, since ultimately, the last thing he wants, is to get an unsatisfactory reputation from one of his 'loyal' and continuing customer. Of course there are some managers who couldn't care less, which in effect, simply means that you'll save both your own time and money by eating elsewhere. Always remember, that the consumer is King, and with so many restaurants to choose from, also understand that you need not settle for either poor service or even worse, inferior tasting food. Dining out should be an enjoyable experience. By following the proceeding advice, you can certainly make it happen quite easily.

—Happy Hours used to be the time of day (usually 4-7pm), when for the price of a discounted drink, you were often treated to as much free food, as you could eat. Well, sad to say, those days are, for the most part—long gone. In its place is a palty $1 off the usual $4 drink price, coupled with perhaps a small discount off the bars formerly 'free' munchies. Bottom line: Todays Happy Hour has been greatly reduced in value, in that the discounts are now so small, that your usually far better off just to go to a restaurant instead. You'll also notice, that many of todays so called 'drink specials', consists mostly of ice coupled with a generic brand of liquor—rather than a premium version. Still, if you happen to live in an area, that really offers a purist's version of the true 'Happy Hour' food fare, (along with their legendary low prices,) then by all means be sure to enjoy the offerings , since it can truly represent a real value. As for the rest of us, we'll simply stretch our dollars further by eating elsewhere. Here's a few (and easy way) to do it:

—Whenever you decide to order a steak at a restaurant, always ask the waiter how many ounces it weighs. I say this, because often times, you'll receive lots of 'sides' (ie bread and salad), yet that will only be coupled with a small (perhaps a 3 ounce) entree of meat. Considering the fact that you might pay $15 or more for $2 worth of beef, you'll certainly want to be sure that your getting the best value for your hard-earned money. Accordingly since meat is normally the most expensive item on the plate, you'll want to get the most of it, as well. Of course, if your on a diet, you'll simply get around this, by ordering the often times lower-priced 'diet special' plate , and thus saving yourself the higher price of the regular meal.

—Perhaps to nobodys surprise, coffee still remains a high profit item at any restaurant—(usually amounting to around $2). Yet nothing quite seems to go with that early morning ham and eggs, like a good-tasting cup of 'joe'. However, during both lunch and dinner, you might want to think twice about ordering your favorite brew. The reason: Not only is the coffee not likely to be brewed fresh,since fewer people normally order it then. You'll also discover, that at many restaurants, instead of getting real 'half and half' with your coffee, you'll instead be served some sort of 'artificial coffee creamer'. Now I don't know about you, but at $2 a cup (plus tax, of course) I only want the best. Sure, you can always go to one of those coffee 'gourmet' shops, but there your favorite brew, will likely cost even more—in fact, nearly three times as much.

Solution: just say no. Instead look for a simple eatery (like a donut shop) where coffee is constantly made fresh. In so doing, you'll likely avoid the expensive-looking restaurant where the so-called 'fresh pot' was most likely made some time ago.

And so here again, you'll discover that being aware of the market can save you some big bucks....even on one of lifes simplest pleasures. And speaking of food and drink items, always ask about any food specials thats currently being offered, which is not listed on the menu. Often times these items will be shown on either the restaurants inside 'blackboard', and/or displayed outside the entrance on a menu style 'sandwich' board. Of course, you'll most likely find such deals at restaurants where large numbers of customers routinely come for lunch. And like any simple profit or loss scenario, many business owners also realize that a restaurants competition is quite fierce, so offering daily 'specials' can literally mean his own financial salvation. Accordingly, thats yet another situation where you can benefit (ie a 'win-win' situation), as well.

Now here's a high profit ploy that you need to be aware of: Valet Parking. This is where a complete stranger takes your keys and then parks your car for a premium charge—and/or tip, as well.

As for using this optional 'service' I simply say two words—'stay alert'. For if you hear the sound of screeching tires from another car that was also being parked by this driver, you might want to settle for simple street parking instead. By doing so, you'll clearly win in two ways. First, you'll save on the extra cost of Valet Parking, and second, you'll know that your car was not mishandled by some employee, who may or may not be around should a problem be discovered (ie scratches on the door, small dents to body, etc.) after you've received the car back Ironically, even at a smaller, yet still popular restaurant, you'll usually have a choice of either free or Valet parking. My advice: always go with the 'freebie'. However, if the parking lot is full, then go with street parking which will either be free (after 6pm), or most likely will require a metered parking fee. Both of which is still far less expensive than Valet Parking would be. Yes…even with parking costs, you also have the choice to either spend or save your money—according to both your wants and needs. Bottom line: bring on the savings wherever they appear—it all adds up!

—Wines: can there ever be a wine which is truly perfect for everyone? Contrary to all those persuasive advertisements, I really don't think so. Yet, if you want to try a glass of wine with your dinner, I suggest that you first try one of the many so called 'House-Wines'. Although, this may be a brand few people have heard of, in many instances, this is the brand that the restaurant is staking its own reputation on with its customers, and thus your quite likely to be satisfied. So go ahead and give it a try. If its not up to your standard, then next time, order the next most expensive wine on the menu, and thereafter continue upward (in price) until you find one that interests you. As with so many other house brands, here too, you have a better than average chance of getting some very good quality for a mere fraction of the competing premium 'name-brand' version. Conversely don't automatically ignore an unknown national brand either, since, after all its really the taste that matters. Just remember that it is the cost of advertising (and over-packaging), that usually makes the real price difference between both of the brands. Bottom Line: by simply taking a chance on the 'cheaper priced' version, the odds are usually stacked in your favor, thereby saving you money while giving you a fine tasting wine to complement that exquisite tasting dinner,—exactly as it was meant to be enjoyed!

—Beers—Now I often wonder which industry has more product on the stores shelves: breakfast cereals or domestic beers. It seems to be, that at certain times of the year, its really hard to tell. Yet, if you want fresh tasting beer with your restaurant meal, you can usually tip the odds in your favor by observing the following:

—initially try the draft (i.e. on tap) beer, since it's likely to be fresher and lower cost than that of its bottled 'cousin'.

—in both instances (whether the brews comes from a bottle or a glass), look for 'hops' rising from the bottom. If you don't see any, chances are the brew is very likely to be old and thus flat tasting—(and you certainly, don't want to pay $4 for that!)

—you might also try looking for a restaurant that serves its beer in a refrigerated mug. And believe it or not, this will normally make the beer far better tasting, even regardless of what brand it is.

—size matters—Its true—some bars offer a 9 ounce glass, while the rest will go the full 12 ounce 'yard',—yet often times at the same price. Always go for the 'big-gulp', since after all the price is identical.

Finally, stay alert in limiting your beer consumption. For although some health organizations believe alcohol (in moderation) can be beneficial to your overall health, alcoholism still remains a big problem today, accounting for more than half of all fatal traffic accidents.

Chapter 10

───────▼───────

How to downsize your tax burden
—a'la carte

When it comes to yearly expenses, perhaps nothing else even comes close to what consumers pay to all levels of government, in the form of taxes. In fact, the very word 'taxation' seems to conjure up an image of financial waste—as clearly it should. Think about this—from the ratification of the US Constitution (1787) to the introduction of the Federal Income Tax in 1913, America got alone quite well thank you, by simply applying only very low duties (ie fees) on certain products. Yet, somehow those minute' fees were adequate enough to provide for the nations defense, the operation of all levels of government, and perhaps most important of all, the freedom of the entrepreneur to grow the countrys industrial infrastructure, into what eventually would become the economic wonder of the free world.

Now perhaps a look into our past, will amplify just how far we've regressed from a country founded on low taxes—into both an over-regulated and over-taxed servant conscripted by all the various levels of bloated government. So let us walk together for just a few moments down memory lane At the time of the Boston Tea Party, (1773), the British applied tax to the colonies was a 'huge' 1%. By comparison, all taxes (local, state and federal) today combined to hover in the 40-50% range. Those rates includes sales taxes, property taxes, income taxes, death and estate taxes, value-added taxes, even gasoline taxes. Now consider this—If you work from the beginning of the calender year, you will need to work almost five full months annually , simply to pay all your taxes. Somewhat ironically, while many workers consider this fact to be oppressive, these same folks also fail to think about replacing the very same people (politicians) who still continue to take their hard-earned money year after year, yet continue to get reelected. What specifically am I talking about? Quite simply this: it is our elected representatives (as well as the various 'feel good' initiatives we vote on), which although might sound 'utopian-like' on paper, instead, amounts to a form of legalized thievery.

For example, how many times have you the taxpayer, been duped into believing that paying more money (in the form of higher taxes) for the public school system would result in a higher quality of 'education?' The answer—FOREVER—(or so it seems). Yet soon after the taxpayers vote approval for the new tax, the schools instead only continue to worsen. Ironically and by way of contrast, statistically the schools with the best testing results come from the states with the LESS amount of taxes. This should prove one simply fact—money alone is NOT the reason for our poor schools. The list of other like-minded social issues can go on and on—voting for a higher gasoline tax in order to solve traffic gridlock. Four years later, the voters find out that their tax money went elsewhere, which had absolutely nothing to do with either building roads or in reducing congestion on the highway. Heres yet another 'tax' ploy—passing a bond measure, in lieu of a tax initiative—(consider that charade as simply a back door tax, which it clearly is), since the interest money that paid to the bondholder comes directly from (you guess it) we, the taxpayers. (Of course, in those 'golden years of yesteryear' that was simply known as a political 'shell game').

Now consider this: In 1998, California voters had just barely passed an increased cigarette tax initiative, that will supposedly go to pay for the health care costs of many smokers, which are now being borne by all tax-payers. However, the problem with this tax, is that it relies on the smokers themselves, to continue to buy cigarettes, since otherwise there won't be enough money to pay for the smokers health costs. In reality, this tax is simply another slick gimmick, since the money is also being used for other issues, thats clearly unrelated to health care costs. Bottom line—the tax is just another ploy in order to separate workers from their hard-earned money. In essence, for some 126 years (1787-1913) the American govern-ment existed without any income tax (except for a few years during the Civil War)—all the while prospering into the wealthiest nation on earth. Yet today, we are shackled by numerous layers of government and wasteful bureaucracies which for all intentional purposes, clearly rips-off.... we, the American taxpayers.

So before I offer some real solutions to not only stopping the escalating tax rates, (while hopefully then reducing it further back,) it should be pointed out that the very presence of a excessive tax system means the gov-ernment ultimately controls, not only how we live , but just as equally important, how much of our money, we finally get to keep.

That fact, (indeed that ISSUE) has been with all levels of government ever since 1913. Accordingly, only when we decide that our taxes are all too confiscatory, (and then act via casting our votes for low-tax politi-cians), will we get, not so much tax reform, but hopefully instead, a long overdue policy of accelerating tax-relief.

As with so many other consumer products and services, we each have the power as to how much we want to pay. However, the major difference with taxes, is simply this: the amount taken from our lifetime earnings amounts to more than all our other expenses combined! Yet folks who will complain about a $1.50 ATM charge being imposed by their bank, will seldom raise their voice anytime ANY tax increase is proposed. The bottom line: Get smart—by getting 'low-tax' savvy!

Ways to downside your own tax-burden Among the numerous ways to reduce your tax burden are the following:

First and foremost, establish a regular IRA retirement account. This will allow you to reduce your annual tax tally, simply by allowing you to delay paying taxes on it, until you withdraw it at age 59 1/2. For example…If your married and make under $50,000 a year, you (and your spouse) can usually deduct $2,000 each year from your gross incomes. In effect, that would then reduce your taxable income to $46,000. (However, with few exceptions, if you take that IRA money out prior to age 59 1/2, you could be hit with both a 10% penalty and interest.)

Now if your in the 28% tax bracket, you will have delayed paying taxes of some $1,120 ($4000 x .28) to the government. This is money that you can now invest, and in so doing, eventually benefit from the 'miracle' of interest compounding!

So if you don't currently have an IRA account, clearly there is no time like the present for starting one. One other point: Now that many mutual funds offer these accounts, look for one that either (a) requires no trustee fee or (b) charges only one fee per account, rather than for each separate fund, since that cost difference can easily amount to several hundred dollars over the coming years.

Avoid paying (high) sales taxes

The easiest way to do this, is to simply buy the item via the Internet. So unless there is a hefty 'shipping and handling charge' added to the purchase price, you can realistically expect to save some big bucks by buying there.

Also, when you go on vacation to one of the few states without a sales tax, you might want to consider buying the item there—that is, if all the other components (ie warranty, quality, national store affiliation) are truly equal. By doing this, you can think of it, as a way of helping to pay for some of your other vacation costs. A few states (and even some localities) also charge a tax on 'dine-in' restaurant meals—but not on food 'to go'. If your state, is one of these, you can cut your costs by occasionally taking your 'restaurant' meal home,—and where you'll also be able to save on the additional cost of any alcohol beverage (or dessert) as well!

Looking for some 'big-time' tax savings? Then always think twice, before you consider buying a new car. The reason: the sales tax on that new vehicle can be a real 'budget buster' if ever there was one. Today the average price of a new car is $22,000. With a 8.25% sales tax, that amounts to over $1800. Now if that's not enough to turn your head, then consider these other costs, which are also associated with that new car purchase:

—Higher interest costs—as a result of the higher loan amount vs. buying a used vehicle (which conceivably might even be paid for with cash)

—Higher insurance costs—that's required to protect both you (and the finance company) if you are involved in an accident

—High maintenance costs—which will most certainly occur once the limited new car warranty expires

Bottom line: Think 'USED' instead—then invest that savings for an even greater return—elsewhere.

Real Estate Taxes—Most people never bother to check whether or not their real estate taxes are correct, but you certainly can by simply going to the local county recorders office to find out what other homes, (which are similar to yours) are valued at locally.

If you should discover that your taxes are higher, you would then want to contact the County Assessors office, to find out why? Such 'investigative' work has routinely save many home owners some SUPER bucks over the years. My recommendation: See also…if 'it can happen to you' Warning: never…but never, should you take the initial assessed value of your home as being the final word. If nothing else, you should always question the tax amount shown. After all, when it comes to the governments money it really is YOUR money, whether you realize it—or not.

Give yourself an instant pay raise

Every year millions of American workers get a income tax refund, due primarily to their own overpayment of taxes to the IRS. This occurs, mainly because the employee claims the wrong number of personal deductions on his W-4 claim form. As a result, the government has full use of this 'extra' tax money for a full 15 months. Now, had you initially claimed the correct number of exemptions, you would of put that surplus money immediately, into your own pocket. How? Well, mainly by allowing the IRS to take fewer dollars out of each paycheck, which then you could have invested for your own benefit, rather than to that bloated (and wasteful) bureaucracy known as Uncle Sam. Now, just think for a moment about all the money you could of invested over the past decades, had you simply taken my advice. Also think about this—as a result of your not having this extra cash when you needed it, how often had you then turned around and had to borrow it from a bank at 18-21%? If your answer was 'more than once', then your loss was even greater. Bottom line:It's time to reverse the tables on the tax man.

So the first thing you need to do tomorrow, is to march yourself down to your companies personnel office and ask them about changing the number of tax exemptions on your W-4 form, so that fewer dollars are being deducted weekly from your paycheck. Once this deduction takes effect, you should then have some 'new-found' money to invest or spend on practically anything you like. Just remember, that you will still owe the full amount of income tax on your yearly income come the following April. Yet the big difference is, you'll have full use of that money…(your money) until then. Think 'investment…interest…income'.

Start a small business—lots of folks do everyday. In so doing, they not only get a chance to become financially independent, they also get Uncle Sam to assist them in reducing their overall tax burden…primarily by allowing for various profit/loss deductions and assorted tax credits. Of course, nobody should start a business just to pay less tax, since they could lose far more in terms of their own principal, than the tax man would take. Yet, its clear that in order for the economy to grow, the government needs to encourage these small business risk takers.

Point of fact: Historically, its been proven that the government itself, benefits even more than the business owner does, since now additional workers are added to the companies tax rolls-thereby increasing overall tax revenue collection to the government. And although most businesses do fail within a few years, still others continue to grow by leaps and bounds into multi-national corporations. The bottom line: if you always wanted to start your own business, begin by first doing some serious business planning, after which you can then go about getting the required financing, in order to get it started.

Then once your totally successful, you will have created an environment where not only have you become financially independent, but you also will take enjoyment from the fact that Uncle Sam helped your along the way.

And since small business is where most of the new jobs are created today, starting one offers you the opportunity for a 'win-win' play. My bottom line: Go for it!

Chapter 11

▼

Tightwad Tips 101—
Ground Zero for the 'need to know' consumer.

It seems, as though everyday consumers are constantly 'confronted' with a wide variety of buying decisions. True, some of these deals are authentic great buys, and even a few have impressive investment potential. Yet many of these are nothing more than so-called 'money pits' that gradually drain your wallet for needless wants and empty purchases. Over time, this money can (and does) amount to a great deal of 'unnecessary' working hours that eventually you will have to do, in order to pay for such 'remorseful' buying habits.

Accordingly, if you've read this book this far, by now you know the 'traps' that I'm talking about:

—the stop and shop(ing) at the higher-priced local convenience store, rather than buying the same product for much less at the nearby super-market.

—buying premium gas for your car, when the lowest cost gas is usually all thats required.

—spending $1 at a soda machine at work vs. bringing your own soda from home—while saving 75% (or more) by easily doing so.

That savings list could go on and on. Here, I simply want to enlighten you to some of the more less obvious money-saving daily expenditures, which if followed, would give you a sizable savings/investment balance for the things that would really add benefit to your life: like travel, investment opportunities, and the inevitable process of retirement planning.

So here then, are several more ways to save on your everyday expenses:

—Hidden Coupons—believe it or not, you'll find these in the 'Yellow Pages', on the back of grocery receipts, as well as inside that jar of morning coffee. Annually, manufacturers distribute BILLIONS of these 'dollars' in the form of coupons, yet less than 2% of them are ever redeemed. (Is it any wonder then, why most Americans have such a low saving rate, when compared to the other industrial nations?

Cigarettes—yes, that 'evil and demonic' product, which the government seems to constantly warns us about (yet, while at the same time collecting BILLIONS in taxes from its sale), has recently risen in price to nearly $5 a pack in some high-tax states—(like California), while selling for several dollars less in its nearby border states—Nevada and Arizona. So if your a smoker (and sometimes visit Reno/Las Vegas/ or even the Grand Canyon) then why not stock up on your favorite brand of cigarettes while there? Think about it—if you enjoy smoking, then why not pay 50% less for the same product, and instead keep the price difference in your own pocket rather than to give it away to some greedy government bureaucracy? Even better—try to quit smoking all together. That way your savings will be 100%.

E-Mail—Question: Why spend .34 cents to mail a letter that not only takes several days to arrive at its destination, but also requires a similar amount of time before a response is received back? By using E-Mail you'll save both time & money. The cost for this service is free—in that, it comes included with your monthly Internet service fee. So if you are looking for a way to cut your communication costs, this is definitely the answer. And, if you believe in the old-adage that time truly equals money, then you'll likely save even more. An added bonus: Use e-mail instead of calling long-distance. In so doing, you'll clearly save an additional 'fistful of dollars', as well.

Reading Glasses—No, I'm not talking about the $100 prescription version, but rather the local drugstore brand which you can buy without a prescription from a doctor.

For a cost of $10-$15 you can instantly improve you reading vision by purchasing these glasses for a mere fraction of what an eye doctor might charge. Of course, this 'tightwad tip' applies only if your vision is not seriously impaired. If it is, than your best bet would be to visit your optometrist for a complete eye exam and/or prescription.

Prepaid phone service—Yes, I know—its convenient and who uses a pay phone today anyway? Well evidently lots of folks still do—for they have come to the conclusion that such a convenience as cellular phone service is simply just too costly for their own budget. At upwards of $20 a month, (plus an additional 'per-call' fee), the annual expense for such a questionable and limited device demands a closer look at a much cheaper alternative—specifically using a coin phone (.35) or even better, a prepaid phone card—(having a $.10-.15 per minute rate). Obviously, if your a light to moderate monthly phone user, you'll save some big bucks by using either alternative—rather than submitting to the usual 'free cellular phone' (WITH MONTHLY SERVICE CONTRACT) ploy, which several of that industries promoters constantly seem to hawk. So if you don't use the phone much, you'll save big by just saying 'no', to all those cellular 'sign me up' offers.

Sundays Newspaper—With TV Guide selling at $2 a copy (plus tax), your much wiser to buy the local Sunday newspaper instead. For not only will the latter have far more information to it (in addition to all those free money-saving coupons), it will also provide you with the same basic information as TV Guide. Likewise consider this: At $2 a week (x 52 weeks), TV Guide will cost you $104 a year. Think you might be able to use that money elsewhere? I know I can—and do! Bottom line:—It's simply time to say 'bye-bye'…to TV Guide!

Travel Magazines—Have you ever needed to book a trip immediately? If so, then you might want to subscribe to any one of the numerous travel publications, thats available today. The reason: you'll likely have immediate (and valuable) information regarding those 'legendary' unpublished discounted fares—and scheduling requirements, which otherwise might take you several additional hours to track down on your own. Sure, you can sometimes access this same information via the Internet—(and sometimes not), but in the case of the travel magazine, you'll be better prepared to comparison shop regarding both the fares and the its related booking requirements. Consider this also: Since Internet fares tend to sell out rather quickly, having an alternative source can make the difference between going somewhere special—or well…simply staying home.

Talk Radio—Hmmm! Let's see, since there's no charge to listen to it, what other benefit could it possibly give me? Plenty—is the short answer. Depending on your subject of interest, local talk radio can literally 'educate' you on any number of various subjects. Let's look at just a few: — Personal Finance—is one such topic that just about every major city in the country has such a radio program. And it's easy to understand why, for here you'll learn about investing from some of the most knowledgeable people in the business. Of course, as always, you must be cautious about their advice, since nobody bats a numerical 1000,—no…not even among such acclaimed 'financial experts' as these folks are. Still their advice on various financial information makes for some very interesting listening. Another area, in which talk radio can save you money concerns the 'do it yourself' business of Home Repair. How?—Well simply from the programs invited guest giving you free information on everything from painting a room to making your home insulation more energy-efficient.

Whats that...you say that your still 'clue less' when it comes to understanding computers? Well relax, for here again, its talk-radio to the rescue, as more and more urban radio stations are providing just such a program for its listeners. So before you spend several hundred dollars on a new computer, be sure to get some basic knowledge of whats available—as well as what you'll actually need. By listening to talk-radio on that subject, it will assist you in that regard. As a result, the information you received there will very likely save you lots of dollars over the coming years.

Finally, there's the subject of Auto Repair. Yes...you can, call that talk-show host and present your own 'technical' questions for an 'on the air' answer, (rather than paying someone else a fee for getting that same identical information). And sure you'll also still need to buy an auto repair manual if you really want to make full use of such knowledge, but at least you will have 'broken the ice' for taking apart some of the 'mystery' of auto repair. Bonus: An added benefit of talk-radio is that it usually appears on the AM dial, where distant reception is usually received much better than that of most FM stations. Translation—you can listen to it at more (and distant) locations, as well.

Restaurant Roulette—In fact, sometimes it might seem exactly like that, whenever you patronize a local eatery, where quantity and quality remain questionable. Of course, a good way to judge whether or not you even want to eat there is to first (and foremost), check the menu thats located outside its main entrance. Here you'll likely find the daily specials which are many times omitted from the higher-priced regular menu found inside. Consumer alert: believe it or not—many times the waiter is not even aware of such 'specials', since often times they've just started their work shift, and have not been told about the 'daily entrees'. So do yourself a financial favor by asking them about any current specials thats currently being touted by the management Heres another tipoff to a good quality restaurant: simply notice how many people are inside it. For instance, if its during lunch hour and most of the seats are still empty, you just might also want to consider an alternative site for lunch. After all, a restaurant that fails to draw people in during its most profitable hours says a lot not only about its food and service—but its overall prices, as well.

Finally, as your walking among the other customers while being seated, try to notice (via a casual glance) the fresh appearance of the food—as well as the portion served. Since after all, $5 today can buy either an ethnic-style buffet smorgasbord—or a palty size quarter pound burger with cola and fries. As always, the bottom line is to remain aware and observant of what your getting for your money. In so doing, the term for such bargains (and slogans)…will then truly become a VALUE DEAL!

Chapter 12

▼

Gimme Shelter—Finding a cure for the housing blues

Housing costs are definitely both a major and fixed cost when it comes to the monthly family budget. Want proof? Then simply pick up any newspaper today and you'll see just how expensive most types of housing can be. For example, In the so-called 'bay area' of San Francisco/San Jose/Oakland (CA), it is not uncommon to see many homes today listed for between $400,000 and $5 million dollars. Of course, even with a low mortgage rate of 6 to 7%, many of these same homes require monthly mortgage payments of several thousands dollars. In fact, this is one of the many reasons why so many high-tech companies which are located here, have such a hard time in finding (or retaining) its own employees. What's also ironic, is that this situation occurs, despite the above average salaries that are paid to the various categories of engineers and other similar white collar professionals. So although those jobs may offer someone great pay, when it comes to paying for those exorbitant housing costs, that area, in effect becomes one of the least desirable to live in. However, if you think this location is alone in such an housing cost imbalance, well…think again. Bottom line: Other large cities(ie Boston, New York, Washington DC—even Phoenix) also have very high housing costs as well.

So what then is the solution to the housing problem? Well, first of all, you need to look at exactly how much housing your monthly NET pay will allow you to spend on shelter costs. Do you remember the old guideline of 25% of your gross pay? If so, then you also know that today that amount is clearly 'passe'. Rather, in many of our larger cities you can expect to pay closer to 50% of your disposable income to go towards housing costs—and thats whether its paid for an apartment rental, manufactured housing, a condo unit, or even that of a conventional home.

Accordingly, once you arrive at a price as to what you can afford to spend, you'll definitely need to shop around first and foremost for location, location, location. Specifically, this could mean moving out to a less populated area, where shelter costs are likely to be substantially less. Of course, you will also need to consider your current salary, in that 'relocation' calculation, in order to arrive at a so-called 'affordability index'. Not surprisingly, you can also expect your paycheck to reflect that lower cost of living as well. As an alternative, you can try to keep that high-paying position in the city, while living for somewhat less in the suburbs—that is, if you don't mind the two hour daily commute, thats likely to be required, in order to accomplish that. Or you can possibly find a lower paying position closer to that new housing area instead. (Unfortunately that will also cancel out the cultural 'amenities' which usually come with living in the big city.) I know…this may sound like a 'wash' (ie one cost/benefit scenario is in reality, equal to the other), but the fact is, most people who live in these lower cost housing locations do manage to own their own homes,—while those living in a higher pay/housing market simply do not. In essence, when it comes to housing costs, a high salary is quite illusionary, once you consider what it will actually buy in terms of home ownership. So be prepared to do the math yourself, since sometimes it pays to stay put, or at least until, the right opportunity comes along. Still at other times, it doesn't. Another point to consider—since there is usually less housing competition in the suburbs (and surrounding rural areas), your thus more likely to get the housing type you want—and at a lower cost, as well.

So lets just say then, that since you've finally decided to consider a move to one of the outlying cities, you'll want to take some necessary follow up action to make sure that whole process of moving goes as smooth as possible. In all candor however, you'll still want to wait a while, so as to investigate the regional schools, the local property tax, and what social activities your new town is likely to offer. Of course, if you need a city-like atmosphere, chances are you will not be happy about living in the 'burbs'. This is certainly one of the main reasons for doing some additional research well before you ever decide to buy. So the best advice that I can give you if your the 'city-slicker' type, is to simply find a temporary roommate, and then share the overall housing costs. At least, that way, you'll get to cut your housing expenses in half, while still maintaining that high paying position. Another option for getting the most value for your housing dollar, is to compare each of the various types of housing costs to each another.

Overall, apartment rentals tend to be the most expensive, especially once you consider that you have nothing left, (other than a rental receipt) when all is said and done. OK, ok...I know, that its also the one housing option with the least amount of work (ie little or no maintenance) thats required by the tenant, since the landlord is ultimately responsible for correcting the majority of housing problems, as noted in your rental lease. Still, the bottom-line remains: you don't own anything that will ever appreciate in value. So as soon as possible, you'll want to but something—anything, that will serve you both as an asset as well as an investment. Accordingly, you'll want to try and visit the surrounding cities for some 'undiscovered' housing bargains, thats ideally coupled with a low-cost financing program. That is, bargains which are in the form of distressed property and thus can likely be 'had' for a low down payment, and quite possibly, won't even be too costly to renovate. Then after living there for a few years, you might want to consider selling your appreciated investment, once the local real estate market turns bullish. However, always remember, that not all property appreciates in value. Many of those five million dollar estates which I referred to earlier, are now selling for one-third (or less) than their former price. Among the reasons: increasing crime rates, an over-priced real-estate market, and/or a loss of jobs, in that area. In many cases however, a house bought today and sold just a few years later, should return a good profit on your original investment. So looking to buy even just a 'fixer-upper' should remain a top-priority, if you truly want to improve your own standard of living, simply by living for less thru lower housing costs.

'Show me the money' was a catch phase from an recent movie—and you might be wise if you also could show some cash to any distressed home buyer, whose also looking to sell as soon as possible. The reason: your more likely to be in a position of financial power when negotiating the buying terms for his distressed property. Not surprisingly, the appearance of cold cash always seems to have a persuasive impact on most sellers. Accordingly, by having such cash, your most likely to come out ahead in any sales transaction. Of course, you'll always want to try to put down as little of a down payment as possible—especially, if you can earn a higher investment rate (i.e. debt reduction vs. your mortgage rate) elsewhere. So all right, you now have you own 'fixer-upper'—and are also paying several hundred dollars monthly in order to meet the on-going mortgage and property taxes. And while all that might seem burdensome, its also Ok, since you now own something of value, which of course is home equity. The next move is for you to think about how you might make a decent profit from eventually selling it sometime in the future (ie 2-5 years). Now assuming that you did your homework correctly,(ie remember its location,location, location that truly matters) you can now realistically expect a profit from its sale, by first getting an appraisal of what your home is truly worth. If its value is too low at this time, simply keep it off the market. By so doing, YOU won't become a distressed buyer, by selling the property at a loss. Don't worry, if the past is any indication, and you have bought a home in the right location most likely the real-estate market will turn in your favor and you should do A-O.K. And speaking of selling your home, rather than give up the usual 6% of its selling price to a real-estate broker, you might want to pick up some books on 'How to Sell a Home' yourself. Ok, I know that it's true, that most of the time people don't even want to look into that option, as they often consider the whole selling process to be far too complicated for the average 'layman' to even understand. Then again, there are many potential sellers who are willing to at least investigate the possibility of trying to 'sell it themselves'.

Now if you fall into the latter category, your savings can actually be quite good. For example, on a $300,000 home, you will have saved $18,000. When you then consider the time involved, that is actually a pretty good hourly rate of return. The bottom line: at the very least, you should purchased a 'how to' book that will help you to decide if its at all possible, for you to sell your own home, yourself.

Now lets 'fast forward' the whole process even further. You've sold the property, made a nice little profit, and now want to repeat the process. Here is where you'll definitely want to be extra cautious. You remember all those surplus over-priced properties I referred to previously? If you paid close attention, you now know that there is something in economics that is referred too as 'the point of diminishing return'. Basically, that is when a product will sell for only so much—no matter how much extra money you decide to put into it. Buyer beware: Try never to buy an expensive piece of property, without realizing the down side of your investment. As an alternative, in most cases, it will be far better for you to buy another low-cost home in an area thats poised for both population growth and economic development.

Accordingly, once you get into the actual process of making a profit, your potential for financial independence, can truly become unlimited.

Clearly, it is then up to you, as to how to invest that money. Some stock options might even offer you an even greater rate of return, so you'll want to consider them as well. The point is, that by buying property over the years (rather than renting) you now are in a position to be financially better off! In essence, real estate deals are just like any other consumer product—they too are negotiable, just make certain that such opportunities are in fact, beneficial to your own financial well-being!

Chapter 13

▼

SCAMS TO SCAN—Now you see it —now you don't

It seems that almost every evening, you can expect to receive a phone call from some 'boiler-room' operation trying to sell you something of absolutely no value. Clearly, the simplest way to handle such calls is to just say no—and then hang up. Yet too often, consumers instead listen to the caller's scripted dialog, as she rambles on about some sweepstakes vacation you've just one, provided of course that you stay at their designated hotel at the usual 'rack' (ie highest) rate. Another common ploy that is offered, is that you are guaranteed to win a stereo system simply by attending a ninety minute lecture on buying into a timeshare. And what a scam that is, since one time just out of curiosity, I took the 'bait' and agreed to attend the…well 'presentation'.

Here's how the scenario went:

First the meeting didn't even start on time, but rather 45 minutes later. Which means that the alleged 90 minute meeting was now 2 hours and 15 minutes. But wait, it got even worse. OK, so then the speaker finally arrives, (yet never explaining or even apologizing for having wasted 45 minutes of our time), introduces himself and then begins the scripted lecture with a few moments of diatribe regarding the time share sales promotion.

Soon after, 'Page 2' starts when he abruptly turns out the overhead lights, pops a sales video into the VCR, and then leaves the room for half an hour or so.

Then after some 30 minutes of client testimonies ('Gee, this timeshare is the best thing that ever to happen to me',) the speaker returns and then asks the group, if their are any questions. There are. In fact their are many, which the video totally failed to address. First up is this question: what exactly is the cost and obligations of the buyer if he rescinds his offer to buy within 90 days of the sales agreement? This is followed shortly afterwards by this question: What can you tell us about the credibility of the development company itself? Lastly, this question is asked—'can you tell us how long has your company been in business?'

The speaker will sometimes avoid answering such 'probing' questions by simply responding that most of those questions can be answered by contacting the company directly. In short, we are given a video-like 'picture perfect postcard' without any knowledge of its actual representation. Of course, due to some other questions now being asked, the 90 minute meeting has suddenly expanded into yet another hour and fifteen minutes to 3 1/2 hours. Next comes the initial sales pitch. This usually comes in the form of a contest drawing, where the winner will possibly reap a $50 savings bond. Of course, the purpose of the 'contest' is simply to get some vital data on each participant, in order to sell both your name and data to firms which might wish to target you for some other related product or service. One last ploy is then presented—the 'one on one' consultation with an 'sales adviser' regarding both the timeshare and your own financial qualification, to secure it. This consumes an additional 30 minutes. (Total time 4 hours!)

Finally, you are led to the 'prize' room where you pick up your free 'gift', from attending the sales presentation. But surprise, what you get is not some quality stereo system consisting of large speakers, a built in carousel-type CD system, or even a dual cassette but rather a $29.95 boom box, which you could of easily bought on sale for half that price. So for 4 hours of your time, in essence you are rewarded at $7.50 an hour. Talk about wasting ones time. Unfortunately, this is but one of the ever-increasing time-bandit ploys that consumers need to watch out for.

Here's several more:

—State lotteries—The odds are far more likely that you'd be hit by lighting before you'd ever win any money by playing such games. However, if you still want to gamble on a long-shot, then try entering a free sweepstakes instead. Clearly, by choosing that option, your only cost will be for a postage stamp. (Just also be prepared for the inevitable onslaught of 'lottery-style' junk mail to arrive soon after that!)

—Charitable Organizations—that you may never of even heard of before. You know the 'scam-operation' type. The random contact where the caller states the group is advocating such and such a cause and would now like you to join them, simply by writing a check (or even worse) giving this unknown caller, your own credit-card number so as to make it even 'more convenient for you'. You probably wouldn't believe how many good intention consumers fall for this trap simply because the caller has appealed to their emotions. Yet, you can protect yourself from that scam, by simply hanging up the phone. In fact, even if you want to give to a known charity, always check it out for complaints, before you send that check along. A good place to start the process would be a call to the local Better Business Bureau and your local consumer protection agency.

—1040 Presidential Campaign Checkoff—Talk about a scam thats qualifies as 'BIG TIME'. This is the little box that appears on your annual 1040 income tax form, and which is usually listed under your name and address. It asks if you would like to contribute several dollars towards the cost of the next presidential campaign. Excuse me, but if everyone said 'no' to this checkoff, does that mean we'd have no such event? I mean from 1776 to about 1976, we never had such a 'choice', and yet somehow those campaigns still went on, and a president was still elected. Some folks mistakenly believe that by checking the form's 'yes' box, that this will make the always required outside fundraising unnecessary. Don't you believe it, as this is witnessed by the everlasting campaign slogan of 'campaign financing reform'. My advice—just say NO! and keep the money in your own pocket or give it to a charity which truly deserves it. After all, the government can take your money any time it wants (via taxes)—and far too often, does.

—'Emotional' Insurance—called it what you will, but what it all boils down to, is simply the 'peddling of fear.' To be specific, I am talking about Cancer Insurance, Accident Insurance, and even Flight Insurance. Now if you want to be covered for all of those concerns, simply purchase a term insurance policy instead. Unlike the numerous exclusions and limitations associated with such 'individual' policies, term insurance will cover you 24 hours a day, 7 days a week. Most important of all however, is the fact that a term policy covers far more conditions than just what those solo policies offer. The premium you'll pay for such coverage is also likely to be lower as well. Bottom line: Go for the Gold by declining the 'specific death' policies and buy the multiple coverage Term Insurance instead. $200 Seminars—Would you believe that you can get virtually the same information from one of these 'exclusive' seminars, simply by purchasing a book by that author, from the local bookstore? It's true. I recently attended one such event for free, (as a incentive bonus from a financial newsletter I'd subscribed to) and which the public had paid $200 to attend. I then took notes of what was said, then check out that authors ($19.95) book, and viola!…there was actually very little difference between the two. Now as a further alternative to attending such high-stakes seminars, you should also check out what the authors competition writes, by reading similar books. In fact, you might not even have to buy the book, once you simply glance thru it. Undoubtedly, you'll quickly get an impression of whether or not it addresses your financial concerns. If it does, then purchase it. In doing so, you will in essence, be investing in your own financial future by always having a referral source, as opposed to just a vague memory of what was said at that expensive 'talk-fest'. Yet another low-cost alternative to that $200 seminar is to watch the numerous money management/investing programs (for free) on TV—and/ or radio. You could then follow up your own interest by attending such low-cost financial planning courses, that are given at your local adult education facility. Thus, for a fee of usually less than $20 you'll likely get some very valuable advice from financial planners and money management professionals. In other words, always start with the least costly source of information(i.e TV programs like Wall Street Week) before spending your hard-earned dollars on some 'prestigious program' which might not even offer you the information you want—or even worse, could lead to your own form of personal 'budget busting'!

—'Overkill' Products—No, this is not the name of some company, but rather a term to describe the so-called 'bells and whistles' on products that you'll never likely used—yet often times pay a premium price for. Example: You want to buy a stereo that will give you a quality sound, when its played at a moderate to high volume. So you go to the local electronics chain store where, what you want, can be had for a mere $150 'buckaroos'. Yet, the salesman all ready knows that he will get a commission based upon the dollars spent on your purchase. Naturally, the more you spend, the more he gets. So not surprisingly, your then shown a more expensive product as he rattles off some 'techno-babble', and which, ironically you have no idea of what he's even talking about. Feeling somewhat both intimidated and pressure by now, your then swayed to purchased the more expensive version. So now instead of the 100 watts of power you originally wanted, you now have 300 watts, which you'll most likely never even use. Clearly, you've just become a victim of the 'Overkill Syndrome'. Unfortunately, this doesn't just apply to stereos, but rather to MOST goods and services in todays marketplace. Know this: In every product made today, there clearly exists a price point which is often referred to as 'diminishing returns'. That is, once your reach a dollar/quality value for what you want, any additional features (ie 'frills) become one of very questionable value. Let me also add, that you don't need to always buy the least expensive version of a product, but rather to question yourself if it's worth the extra price to pay for such frills. Most of the time you'll discover its not. Case in point: How often have you read about a consumer 'Best Buy' that offers both quality and price thats been rated superior to some other higher priced national brand and which costs several times more? If 'seldom' is your answer, then I suggest that you buy the latest consumer buying guide. Within its pages several versions of various products are offered, yet all appear to highlight the numerous products which meet their qualifications for a 'Best Buy' rating. This is certainly one of the best ways to 'save' money—(and/or to invest it!) So always 'think twice' before you and your money part ways, by simply asking yourself: 'Is it a Want (national brand) or a Need (basic function item)?'

'Off-Line' Investing—Hello…is anybody home, that wants to invest in stocks, who has NOT heard of a computer of even a digital telephone? Clearly, with either device today, you can shave 50-75% off the cost of buying and selling stocks. Happily, it seems that even many 'on-line' investment services are getting more and more 'user-friendly' for the novice, who is looking to get rich quick 'the old-fashioned way', via investing in the profitable stock market. Yet even for those, who don't want to self-learn the basics of trading, you can still talk live to a broker for a much higher cost than basic 'on-line' trading involves. And if the purchase of a computer system for 'on-line' trading seems as if it might cost too much, then simply try this low-cost alternative for trading: your digital home phone. In essence, by responding to the phones 'scripted options', you can accomplish much the same transaction as with the computer. True it will sometimes cost you a few dollars more to trade, but it will still be some 50% less than doing a trade via a live broker. Just remember, that regardless of which trading mechanism you choose you are still personally responsible for the total transaction costs.

Now consider this 'bit' of advice to be part of my 'Trading 101' course: First, always try a few small paper trades before going 'live' with your own real money, just to see how well (or poorly) you would have done. Then once your success confidence builds up, you can then invest in a home computer to expand upon your stocks portfolio. Either way, you now have a tool in which to pocket a minimum of 50% savings over those traditional broker trades. Now thats what I call a rate of return, that's clearly just begging to be taken advantage of!

—Moving Companies—When you consider that most people relocate every several years, you might assume that from such experience, would come a knack for knowing how to save dollars when comparing rates among the various and competing carriers. Yet, it seems that instead of looking for ways to cut their own costs,(ie renting a do-it-yourself truck rental) these same consumers continue to give their moving business to the big-name carriers. Sure, there's a good reason (ie less stress) for hiring someone to do all the heavy lifting thats required of a family move. But clearly there are also several money-saving alternatives. Number 1 would be to sell what you don't want (or need) to move simply by conducting 'a garage sale'. By setting aside one weekend, you'd be surprised at what you could sell—thereby putting some extra money in your pocket. A second benefit of the garage sale would be that you won't have to take the time to wrap that specific item for moving—since now that its been sold. Still another source for you to consider is donating your items to a charitable organization, while at the same getting a tax-deduction in the process. Thus, with those three options geared towards reducing your quantity of goods to be moved, you hopefully have eliminated the need for hiring a large carrier. In so doing, you also have just kept several hundred dollars in your own pocket. Simply by hiring students, friends, (and/or even by 'doing it yourself'), you can get your possessions moved for less, via renting a rental truck instead. However, if you still decide that its too much trouble and still want to go with a carrier, then call around and always compare rates. Consider also those relatively 'unknown' advertised companies listed in the yellow pages, even if its a name you don't immediately recognize. Needless to say, competition among the many independent moving companies is fierce in this business, so always make sure that the company your considering has been in business for at least a few years and that no major complaints have been filed against them, within the time period. Of course, you will also want to be sure that their insurance coverage is at least compatible with its name brand competitor, just in case, you need to file a claim for either loss or damaged goods. So whether you do it yourself or hire a 'independent' carrier, you'll save some serious money when it comes time to pull up stakes—via 'moving on'.

—'We Won't Be Undersold' is an attractive sales slogan retailers like to advertise, however a new ploy has recently emerged that all too often, consumers are still unaware of—namely, a 'restocking fee' of 10-15% on any merchandise that you returned to the store. The idea for such a fee is two fold. First, it was initiated primarily to discourage merchandise returns—and two, it serves as another source of income for a retailer looking for some additional profit advantage over the competition. Unfortunately, such restocking fees has been most prevalent in the 'fast-moving' electronics retail industry. For example: as a lure to get a customers business, some stores will often times advertise a low price (ie loss leader) product (ie 19' color tv for $99) and may or may not limit the quantity each store has for sale. As a result, the store has initially enticed the consumer with the low price—but once the customer visits the store, he is now offered a higher price alternative instead—a process, that is known as 'bait and switch'. Of course, during the sale transaction, it is unlikely that the salesman will ever mention the restocking fee,—that is, unless you do. However, more times than not, consumers don't even realized that such a fee exists,-that is, until they decide to return the product. Consider this scenario: suppose you buy a $1000 computer, then decide that for whatever reason, you want to return it to the store for a refund. Your restocking fee in this case could easily amount to $150. Of course, if consumers were previously aware of that, then few of them would ever shop at that store. Accordingly, that's exactly why you need to take the initiative and protect yourself—by simply asking for the stores printed return policy—before you buy. Once you realize that you could be 'financially penalized' for making a simple mistake (or even from simply changing your mind), you'll clearly want to avoid that retailer—even regardless of how low his prices might appear to be. Bottom line: consumers should expect value on everything they buy. Charging a restocking fee, violates that premise and is a clear rip-off. Your best bet: avoid shopping in any store that charges one.

—Hospital Emergency Room's—are often times fill with patients who very rarely have a true life-threatening injury. As a result, such patients (or most likely, their health insurance carrier) are charged higher fees, than would of been charged at one of the local '24/7' (ie they are always opened for business) medical care centers. Unfortunately, the usual belief among the public, continues to be that since the patient is paying premiums for the medical insurance anyway, he should fully benefit from it by simply using it—regardless of how minor his physical injury might be. That 'belief' of course has a 'flip side'—namely an eventually higher insurance premium. However, there is another alternative (and even lower-cost option) to both the medical center and the ER, and that is to first determine how extensive is your injury. Thus keeping a family medical guide handy is not only a cheap way to quickly diagnose the injury, but is also very helpful in applying some basic 'first-aid' treatment according to the remedy that's suggested for that injury. For example, if you have symptoms that are indicative of having the flu,(which believe it or not...is a common complaint of ER patients during the cold season), you can easily flip thru the medical guide for both the flu's symptoms as well as its stated home treatment remedy. In addition, the cost difference between such a 'preventative' guide and being treated at an ER for such a minor 'illness' can easily amount to $75-$100,—and that's every time you visit either an ER or other medical center. Now consider this: If you visit an ER as little as four times a year for minor injuries/illnesses, you are essentially paying $400 (or more) than is really necessary. And even if your insurance carrier is paying for it, your own premiums are likely to be increased as a way to simply reflect that charge. The message here is to only use the ER ,for what it was intended for—namely, a serious, life-threatening condition, for which there is no other possible alternative. So leave the 'minor' illnesses to either the lower-cost medical center, or preferably to the professional information that you've extracted from the medical guide. Bottom line: If your looking to save several hundred dollars a year in medical bills, this is clearly one way to do it!

—Hospital Charges—for professional medical treatment is one category where the patient is pretty much at the total mercy of the doctors. Yet there are other charges applied to your hospital bill which you should also be aware of, and which are also grossly over-priced when compared to what that same item sells for outside the hospital. What items am I talking about? Well…for starters, there's aspirin. For example—just recently a local drugstore chain advertised a 500 tablet bottle for $2, (thats less than a penny an aspirin.) Still, the hospital would certainly charge you far more than that, thus increasing your costs while increasing their profits—by some several thousand percentage points. This same process also applies to hospital supplied soap, razor blades, shaving cream, even band aids. Of course, although the retail cost of these and similar incidentals is usually quite reasonable outside the hospital, you…as a patient are expected to pay an excessive premium for all of them,—regardless of whether they are requested by you…or not. A much better way to 'treat' these high prices, is to plan accordingly by simply providing your own products from home. If you think this won't save you much money, then take a close look at the next hospital bill you receive. It should clearly detail every item. If it doesn't then immediately contact the hospital billing department for that information. Clearly, anytime a consumer can reduce his medical cost, (in such an easy manner like this) is one of the best investments around today. You can expect a return on such medical 'savings' of 500-1000%.

Conclusion: that is a rate of return that few stocks (if any) could match, and is also 'risk-free' to boot!

—10-10-XXX Long Distance Carrier Plans—Tired of being bombarded with an endless charade of TV commercials and 'junk-mail' flyers that hawk the merits of a companies long distance phone calling plan? If so, then you might want to investigate the fine print of many of these 'money-saving' offers, long before you decide to sign on the dotted line. And just like Sherlock Holmes, you too will likely discover several startling surprises, once you uncover the 'hidden' truth. First, you'll realize that the low rate (ie 5 cents a minute) thats advertised, often times applies only to the first thirty days of service. After that, each call will likely double (or even triple) in price. Add in the monthly service charge (another $5 to $10) and the minimum number of calls thats required to get the 'low-introductory' rate, and suddenly you realize that the much-herald 5 cent a minute call is actually costing you closer to 25 cents (or more) per minute. In fact, when you also include the numerous local, state, and federal taxes to your phone bill, you'll likely pay anywhere from 300 to 1200% more, than you were initially led to believe.

No way, did you say? Well then, if your looking for a better way to cut your phone costs try purchasing a 'prepaid phone card' instead. Merely by dialing around with the local merchants,you can usually find some cards that offer a 'true' 10 cents (or less) per minute phone rate, which even includes all the taxes and surcharges, as well. Ironically, all three of the major long distance carriers also offer their own phone cards, yet they often charge you an additional fee (from $1 to $3) each time you use it, thus making their so-called 'competitive' rates truly 'bogus'. Of course, an even better way to make a long-distance phone call, is via your personal computer. So long as you have speakers (and the appropriate software), you can call long-distance and chat at an even lower cost, than if you were using a prepaid phone card. Thus if you make a lot of such calls, you can easily expect to save several hundred dollars a year, simply by using this 'advanced' form of telecommunication. That in effect, IS the 'true' low-cost alternative to using '10-10-XXX!' So try saying 'adios' to the costlier 'Big-Three'…and say 'Hello'…via the Internet!

Environmental Products—is undoubtedly one of the biggest consumer 'rip-off's' of all times. For example: don't you just love to read about more taxpayer money going into yet, another environmental program, that once again promises to attempt to remedy the very same problem which has existed since they received their first dollar, via our taxes? A case in point: the clean up of toxic waste (ie Super fund). That program has been in existence for over a quarter century, and still less than 15% of the designated polluted sites have ever been cleaned up-even though, we the taxpayer has poured literally billions of tax dollars, in order to remedy the problem. Of course, the Super fund is not the only 'rip-off' to be found under this category—here's several more:

—Low-flush toilets. These require 1.6 gallons of H20 per flush. That's nearly one quarter the amount of water needed for the previous generation model of toilets. Now for the many who yearn to be 'environmentally correct' it sounds as though, such a low-flush unit would actually conserve water while saving the homeowner some serious money—especially since many such toilets also come with a $75 mail-in rebate. Still the reality of this scam can found in the daily newspaper. In fact, heres a recent headline, which seems to say it all—'Consumers demand the return of old Faithful'. That message is quite simple: The newer units don't always flush away all that is…well…lets just say…unsightly. As a result, the so-called 'low-flush' has to be flushed three—or even four times, thus clearly resulting in no true savings at all. Sure you might get a rebate of $75 bucks in the mail, but also think of the inconvenience that you need to consider, by having to repeatedly 'address the problem'. And to add insult to injury, just try and imagine what your house guests might think once they need to visit 'nature' and discover the 'inefficiency' of your 'new and improved' toilet. No thanks…but as for me, I too prefer the old-style toilets back,—and as the saying goes—'sooner rather than later.'

Here's yet another environmental 'rip-off' thats often promoted in various cities—recycling plastics. Although most consumers aren't away of it, plastic containers come in various chemical compositions, which don't always interact with one another, thereby making some plastic containers economically unfeasible to recycle. Accordingly a grading system has since been set up, so as to keep plastics of a certain type within that same recycling category. For those 'in the know', the various category types can be found on the containers 'south side', and normally runs with the numbers 1 thru 6. For the most part, #1 plastic is mainly food containers, yet food is also packed in #5, a sturdier plastic that normally is not recyclable. Thus it ends up in the local landfill and adds to the mountain of waste that is still being discarded daily from around the world. You might even see an advertisement asking the consumer to recycle its products container, yet ignoring the fact, that no such facility even exists. Bottom line: the maker of the 'recycled' product gets good public-relation (PR) marks for being 'environmentally aware', yet in reality is actually raking in an additional profit simply by further adding to the waste stream.

Ironically, there are still many other 'environmentally correct' products which in reality only waste precious natural resources—and tax dollars. Perhaps the biggest component of that scam, is the mass transit systems of many cities, and which traditionally have a low ridership record as well. Sure, its hard to imagine one of the big eastern seaboard cities like Washington, New York, or even Boston functioning without such systems. That's all well and good—but what about many Western cities like San Jose or LA? Granted it will take some time for these fairly new systems to catch up to their eastern counterparts in term of daily ridership, but in many cases, these systems will never...ever, payback the taxpayers who foot the bill. Of course, there are other reasons as well, for this transit ploy. Primarily though, it results from the western US's love affair with the automobile—and the vast open spaces to which no other form of transportation exists. Add in the issues of scheduled delays, poor maintenance and urban crime, (which are committed almost daily on some of the more densely populated transit systems) and its not surprising why overall ridership continues to remain rather low. Yet, at the same time, (at least for many vacationers and visitors), mass transit remains one of the best transportation values for getting around in a major city. Since these visitors only pay a direct fare when they use the system, they are, in effect benefiting from such transportation—while its own taxpayers, clearly do not. Now to add insult to financial injury, both the bus and light-rail systems often compete with one another (ie even along the same route) for that same small (and declining) group of local riders. The bottom line: county taxpayers get more air pollution and higher taxes thats literally wasted for what is essentially a financial 'white elephant.' Bottom line: the real purpose of such a 'bogus' transit system is to create jobs for the related (and powerful) special interests groups, like unions and the so called environmental 'protection' groups. Taxpayers it seems…are always considered last.

Publications—of all types still continue to thrive, even today in the era of the Internet. In essence, just about every magazine can be offered (and is) to the public at a lower cover price than whats often found on the newsstand—via subscription rate. Therefore if, your a routine reader of a certain magazines, you'll definitely want to order a subscription—and thereby have your money earn the equivalent (tax-free) saving rate of 50-75%. If you think, that the amount of money saved is somewhat minuscule, then consider this: A weekly magazine that sells for $3 (plus tax), will cost you about $160 a year. If you can save 75% (via a subscription), that amounts to $120. If you then invest that amount in equities paying just10% a year, over time that 'small savings' will amount to several thousand dollars. And all that it really 'cost' you was to simply pay less for the product-via calling their toll-free number. So try never to pay the full cover price for any magazine that you intend to buy more than once. And even if you don't want a subscription, then try instead one of the national bookstore chains that offers a standard10% discount on most books and magazines.

Here's still another way to save even more: simply share a subscription (and its cost) with a friend—and then when your finished with it, give it to a charity—for a possible tax deduction. All in all, thats a true 'win-win' situation!

High Priced Theme Parks—If you have kids, you already know the ones I'm referring to. Quite simply, they are the national ones, whose prices seem to predictably rise every year. At present a one day ticket cost will amount to about $50 per person, at such parks. Now for a family of four thats $200—and EXcludes such incidentals as parking fees, concession food (and souvenirs), and selected 'optional' services (like having your child's portrait drawn by an in-park artist.) Thus, a more realistic amount for just a few hours of 'entertainment' can easily amount to nearly $300. Yet, if you think you have to settle for such exorbitant prices, think again. Instead, for just a few dollars you can treat the whole family to a very enjoyable outing at the County Fair. There you'll experience many exhibits (ie arts and crafts), many of which are usually produced locally. Of course, the kids will have numerous rides to try out, several of which are usually new in theme…each year. In addition, the expense for 'eats' will also cost less, In fact, sometimes you might even be treated to seeing a live band there performing for free, during the dinner hour. Don't be surprise however, to find out, that the total bill for all this variety amounts to only $75—for a family of four—a saving of $225 over that 'name-brand' (and often times longer line theme park). OK…ok, it's also true that while most County Fairs only last a few weeks, their counterparts are opened six-months or longer each year. Now if you want variety between the different fairs, the solution is to simply travel to another nearby County Fair. Since no two Fairs are ever exactly the same, you'll still come out ahead by avoiding the higher-priced theme parks. In fact, some cities even offer their own 'specialty parks', (as well as the more informative natural and historical museums), in order to compete with 'the other guys' entertainment. In most cases, these alternative and historical centers are truly a 'best buy' for the real value, which they routinely deliver. OK then…but what if your kids just won't accept a substitute for the so-called 'real thing'? Then the obvious solution is to simply look around for a discount coupon off those high-ticket prices. Accordingly, here's a list of where your likely to find them: On the back of soda cans; from a promotion at the local fast-food outlet; on the back of your grocery receipt; in the 'coupon' section of the yellow pages phone directory; inside the national entertainment discount book; inside the local paper's weekend entertainment section; coupons offered thru your local credit union, on the side of a grocer's brown bag, and finally, believe it or not—even in your daily pile of throwaway junk mail. Of course, the savings from these 'money-saving 'coupons' can usually amount to 25%—or more. So if the County Fair and /or cities own theme parks simply won't do, then check around, as these 'other' savings can be quite substantial.

Furniture Kits—Glance at many daily newspapers today and your likely to see either a TV/Stereo or Home Theater furniture cabinet, that you can just imagine, would fit nicely in your own home. Then you notice the price—$49, and think for just a moment what a great buy that is. Unfortunately, you then notice in the small print, those two most dreaded words which many consumers tend to avoid—'Assembly Required'. In essence, this means that you will need to devote some 7 to 10 hours in trying to put the unit together. Now if you think that task is easy, then you'd be wise to think twice before purchasing one. For such kits are in fact very difficult to assemble either due to their many small parts, (which ironically are sometimes missing from the carton or often times gets lost soon after) to those 'difficult to understand' technical drawings (and instructions), which so many 'do it yourselfer's', soon find to be both utterly confusing and time consuming. True, some stores will offer an extra assembly charge to provide the labor, but often times even that turns out to be not as exact as buying the unit already made. As a result, the cost difference between an unassembled and complete unit is likely to be 200% higher than that $49 so-called sale suggests. The bottom line: Even if you consider yourself to be a 'Jack of all Trades', your still likely to be better off buying the unit fully assembled. Think of it this way: If your time is worth $20 an hour and it takes you ten hours to assemble one of those units, that means an additional $200 is added to the advertised cost of that $49 price tag. Had you instead paid the $149 retail price of the assembled unit, you'd be $100 ahead,—and saved yourself unlimited frustration to boot. Finally, if even that price is still too high, then look in your local paper (or phone book) for used furniture. Also keep a lookout for 'estate sales'—as that's one option where you'll often find quality furniture for just pennies on the dollar.

Luxury Items—Have you ever been among the first to purchased a newly developed product, simply to say that you own 'such and such' an item? If you have, then you also realize that shortly thereafter, many of that items 'unique' characteristic soon become incorporated into its lower priced version. (In many cases, it often is extended to the basic model as well). Bottom line: Never be among the first to buy any new upscale product. The reason: First, you'll pay a premium for it, and second you will in essence become a 'guinea pig' for testing out any undiscovered bugs that will have develop along the way.

Heres an example: When the VCR first came out. it was advertised with plenty of 'bell and whistle' features. Yet within a year, most of those same features had become available on the cheapest models as well. Had you instead waited for those feature to filter down, you could of saved yourself several hundred dollars, in the process. Another example: When the Chevy Vega first hit the market, it was actually considered to be the first real competition for foreign small cars. Soon after however, the car gained a reputation for numerous mechanical problems and unreliability. Now, had you waited just a year or two after the car came out, you would of realized that this was not a car you would have wanted to buy. In effect, you would have saved yourself both money and agony over having purchased one.

Although many manufacturers would like us to believe that the highest priced version of a product is the best thats available, its simply not true—most of the time. Think about this: If your a company that wants to make the most profit on an item, would you produce a luxury car or a so-called 'mainstream' model car? Although, the price profit would be greater on the former, the higher profit would actually come from more of the latter cars being sold in volume. Not only that, but a company knows that in order for it to stay in business, it must satisfy the mass market. Therefore, both the testing and improvement of these lower priced products are usually given the companies top priority, in terms of both quality control and reasonable pricing. Bottom line: the best made products are usually found in products made for the mass market. Items which are priced for the luxury market, are seldom worth the extra cost demanded of them. So instead of wasting your hard-earned money on some 'icon image item' shop instead for products which offer real value in both price and quality. In time, your investment portfolio will thank you for doing so.

Chapter 14

▼

EDUCATIONAL COSTS—Up, up and Away

Few expenses are more conscious to the consumer today, than financing a college education, whether it be for their own children or even for themselves. It thus comes as no surprise, that almost every year, educational costs exceed the rate of inflation—and often times by 50%—or more. Of course, you have undoubtedly heard about the Ivy League schools of the Northeast (ie. Harvard, Princeton, Yale etc.) charging some 300-400% higher tuition (and fees),than state institutions, yet you also know that each of these Ivy-league schools, could easily charge even more and still not meet the demand for their services. So what then, is a parent or student to do in the face of such financial burden? In a word—PRIORITIZE. You know, this is that one word that creeps into your conscious mind, whenever a monetary choice needs to be made. It is also the one word that weaves it's way throughout this book, simply because it represents the great dividing line between having money most of the time—or having very little, due to ones own hindsight when deciding between a want and a need. Clearly, in the education arena, this is even more apparent. Now, this does not mean to suggest (or even imply) that no one should not go to a prestigious college simply due to the higher cost, but rather that you should be financially prepared to possibly sacrifice certain things, in order to do so. Of course that upscale college expense might be worth it to you, especially if you end up with a high paying position, due in part to your resume credentials noting, that you have in fact, graduated from such a 'world-renowned' school.

So for anyone considering such a school, the first and best advice would be to start saving early—as well as, in applying for the various types of financial aid, which might be available. Of course, most of this assistance would come under either a loan or grant program. In fact, depending upon what information you enter on your aid package application, it is quite possible that your own out of pocket costs could even be significantly reduced to an affordable level. Yet, until you apply for financial assistance, you won't know if your even qualified for such aid. Therefore, you should apply as soon as possible, since the funds that are available are often times strictly limited by Congress. Since almost every college today has a financial aid office, you will want to make an appointment with them, upon your initial decision to attend that college. It is also important to note that even if you do receive financial aid during your first year, you will still have to apply each and every year after that. So depending on your own monetary situation, you will want to make certain that your have sufficient 'backup' assets, in order to pay the costs,(and thus continue your education) should your application for future aid be denied.

Now for those of you, who might not qualify for such assistance, there are currently two new tax credits available from the federal government in addition to a tax-shelter vehicle, known simply as an Education IRA!

Here then is a summary for each of the three tax-credit programs:

First and foremost is whats known as the HOPE credit. This basically allows you to subtract $1000 for the first $1000 spent on both school tuition and fees during your first two years at the school. A $500 tax credit is then applied to the next $1000 during those same two years as a freshman and sophomore. This will give you a total credit of $1500. So if your cost for two years of college was $2000, you've just reduced it by 75%. This credit also requires that you be enrolled at least half-time, yet there are no age restrictions on its qualifying requirement. Accordingly for a married couple, their total gross amount must be under $80,000 in order for them to each take the full $1500 tax credit. One note of caution however is this: the credit begins to phase out after certain income limits are crossed. For example, if your single, once you reach the $40,000 gross income bracket, the credit is reduced. If you exceed $50,000, the credit immediately disappears.

Still another tax credit program is whats known as the LIFETIME Learning Credit. Unlike the freshman/sophomore restrictions of the HOPE tax credit, this alternative offers anyone a 20% tax credit (i.e. $1000) on the first $5000 spent on tuition and fees. (After the year 2002, this 20% credit will be expanded to the first $10,000 spent on such costs). However, the same income limits apply to this program, as they do to the HOPE credit. Still, it offers any student (adult or otherwise) a tax credit regardless of their age. So even if your a college graduate already, you will qualify for this credit—providing of course, that your own income qualifies you as well. Bottom line: if you have ever wanted to return to school, in order to make either a career change or maybe to even learn an additional vocation, this program could in fact, make it happen.

The last program you should know about is the Education IRA. This allows up to $500 per year to be set aside for your childs post-secondary education. Basically, that amount is deducted from your gross income at tax time. However, it's phase out begins at the $160,000 for a married couple and $110,000 for single filers. Ironically, aside from the very low tax benefit of this program, another minus appears—namely, that you will not qualify for either the HOPE or LIFETIME Learning Credit, in the same year when you receive the benefit of that IRA distribution. You also must stop contributing to the program when your child reaches 18. By age 30, if there is still money in the account, it must be transferred to a younger member of the family. Otherwise it will need to be withdrawn—with taxes paid, on the unspent amount. Not surprisingly, few consumers have taken an interest in this program. Which tends to explain why yet another saving vehicle needed to be introduced in Congress. In the tax-reform bill of 1997, that vehicle became known as a Roth IRA savings account. This plan simply allows you to pay the full taxes now, which would normally be due to the government upon your retirement. (The traditional maximum saving limit of $2000 for a tax-deductible IRA also applies here.) However, the downside to this program is simply this—there is no tax-deduction and earnings are only tax-free if you withdraw them after age 59 1/2. Although you can withdraw the money earlier (for example to pay for education expenses), you would still have to pay taxes on the accumulated earnings. The basic difference between a traditional IRA and a Roth IRA, is that the former delays paying the taxes due, while the latter does not. However, the main benefit for the Roth IRA holder means that no tax is due upon withdrawal after age 59 1/2. Depending upon your own personal situation, a Roth IRA may or may not be beneficial to you. Clearly, the best way to figure if it is, would be to consult a tax professional or merely sit down and number-crunch the figures yourself.

ADDITIONAL COSTS

Although tuition and fees make up the largest amount of college costs, there are associated expenses, which can bust any students budget, if he fails to shop wisely while being enrolled. Foremost among these is room and board—for although students have the option of living on campus, it is usually much cheaper for them to live at home, while attending a nearby college. Sometimes however, student housing is also a wise choice, since many of these units will offer a kitchenette, in order to further reduce your housing/living expenses. Still, an even better way is to find a roommate, rent a large size apartment or condo, and then split your total housing costs by half. One final note however: be sure that any lease that you sign is no longer than your expected school year (i.e. 9 months or 1 year if you intend to enroll in summer school). Otherwise, you'll be legally required to pay for the time when your not there.

Computers—Once upon a time, the cost of these units was in the thousands of dollars. But at the present, a very powerful desktop computer can usually be had for only a few hundred dollars. And considering the applications which a computer can perform (i.e. spreadsheets, word processing, e-mail, etc), this product clearly qualifies as a 'best buy', for todays college students. Yet even before you buy a computer system, you will want to check out the schools own computer center and find out what type of operating system it uses. That system will be either a PC (DOS)—IBM type unit, or a Macintosh-based system (for Apple brand models.) Since the two operating systems are not compatible, a disk written in one format will not help you if it is then unreadable due on a completely different operating system. Accordingly, it would be wise to purchase an computer system that is identical to that of the schools own system, so that you can then use a similar formatted 'floppy' disk, when working on it while at home. Although, you can often buy a computer at a discount on campus, you are more likely to find a better deal off-campus, by simply searching the weekend edition of your local newspaper. And remember to also get the best (and longest) repair warranty thats available. Otherwise, any future repair cost, might likely end up costing you even more money than purchasing a brand new unit would.

A much different version of the PC arrives in the form known as a 'laptop'. In essence, this computer offers both convenience and flexibility, of which no desktop unit can match. For example, it can be carried to lectures or the library, thus making its true portability its principal selling point. In addition to costing a great deal more than their desktop 'cousins', these units are also subject to both severe abuse and random theft. However, if you can accept these negatives, then you have plenty of choices (and prices) in todays marketplace. Bottom line: you should try never to leave these items unattended. In fact, most of the same buying rules that were previously mentioned for desktop computers applies to the laptop, as well. Additionally, since these units are more fragile than their desktop 'cousin', you will also want to give some thought regarding any type of 'Extended Warranty' that might become available for purchase with such units. If possible, have it also insured under your homeowners policy, for unlike the lower-priced desktop, the laptop still manages to demand a premium price—even in todays 'surplus-like' marketplace.

Used Text Books—Did someone say used? Yes….and most definitely do we, especially when one considers the ever-escalating prices for college text-books today. Now consider this 'bit' of information as simply Economics 101: you can easily purchase used books from two sources—the campus book store, where the usual book discount is about 25% (or less) from prior students who have since finished the course, and now want to get some greenbacks returned on the books original purchase price.

Yet before you buy at either place, be certain of these two things:

First—that the current edition of the book will in fact, be used in your class, and second, that the condition of the book is at least in good condition. Otherwise, any used book purchase would likely be a complete waste of money.Still another source of used textbooks, is the campus bulletin board. Here your likely to find exactly what your looking for—and at a price thats much lower than your likely to find anywhere else, (including that schools used bookstore).

Of course, the only time to get the best selection of books, is at the beginning of the school year—for not only will you then get the selection of books from last years student, but also from the newer students, who have since dropped out of the course—for whatever reason. And with some (new) school books now demanding almost $60 per subject, you can easily cut that cost, by buying used.

Finally, to cut your costs even further always try to sell your own books, once you finish the class, as well.

Transportation Costs—If your a student, then think 'mass-transit' for one of the best deals in commuting costs today. The reason: many transit systems currently offer a student-discount pass, which allows for unlimited rides on both the bus and light-rail systems, usually even on a 24/7 (ie anytime) basis. Of course, if you purchase a monthly pass, the cost per ride goes down even further still. Clearly, when one considers the escalating cost of both gas and car insurance, a student monthly transit pass is easily the best way to go. So even if you own a car, you still might want to choose this alternative, simply in order to cut down on your cars wear and tear, as well as the daily drudge of having to drive in 'stop and go' traffic.

In addition, many schools today also charge parking fees to use their lots, so theres yet another reason (ie expense) to leave your car at home. Conversely, if you can car pool with someone, your costs would then likely be somewhat compatible to that of the mass-transit pass, in which case, the convenience of taking your own car would likely be worthwhile. This is especially true, if you take night courses, when transit schedules are much less frequent, and ironically, somewhat less dependable as well. The bottom line: look into both options, then decide which best suits your own particular transportation needs.

State Colleges—are no longer a 'Best Buy'—but rather a better buy than many private colleges are today! For example: Do you remember when there was a wide cost difference between the tuition charges at a state college and that of a private institution? If so, then you now know, that such times have change, and while the costs still continues to advance at many private schools today, most state colleges have also greatly increased both their own fees and tuition rates as well. Still, there can be little dispute that a state college continues to offer a 'good' (if no longer great) deal, for ones educational dollars. However, be aware that this fact applies only to 'in-state' students. Conversely, for those attending such schools, as residents from another state, the costs can easily be as much (and sometimes more) as attending a local private college at home might be. For example, some state colleges will charge five times as much in tuition costs for non-residents as they do for their in-state students. In essence, this amount is very close to the total cost of attending a private university, at home. So if you have the chance to choose between the two (public vs. private) colleges, you should go with the school which not only has the curriculum program you want, but also has the academic reputation for excellence, as well. And believe it or not, this latter point can eventually mean several thousands dollars to you over the years, simply because your resume has a distinguished (ie Ivy league) schools, name on it.

Yet, there are many state schools that also offer a quality education, are known as being quite reputable, and are also highly respected among both the business and academic community. So if you are interested in getting the best value for your educational dollar, be certain to check out all the options, since the 'right' decision here, can mean a huge monetary difference over your lifetime. One final note: always be sure to look into Community Colleges, since you can attend there for the first two years (at less cost), than those same two years would cost you at a four-year state college. In addition, most state schools will also accept your transfer credits from the community college, yet always verify that fact in writing (from the state college), before you take the course. Heres another bonus in attending a community college: Your housing and transportation costs are likely to be lower as well. The reason: since there is no housing available on campus, living at home will undoubtedly be somewhat cheaper than renting an apartment. Transportation costs are also likely to cost less, since there are several community colleges spread throughout every state, thus making one fairly close to where you live. In essence, it is the Community College (rather than the State College), that is likely to offer you the best value for your academic dollar, so be certain to check out what they have to offer. For who knows, the 'real deal' for that prized education, might even be right there—in your own hometown.

ALTERNATIVES TO COLLEGE—Vocational, ROTC,—and even AmeriCorps!

It isn't too often that you hear about either of the above alternatives. when the topic of secondary education comes up. Yet according to various labor statistics, all of these options are among the most promising, for anyone not contemplating direct admission into a four-year college program.

The reasons for this are numerous:

First, not everyone has an interest in pursuing a college degree. Rather, some students would prefer to learn a technical skill through either a vocational education course or even an 'on-the-job' training program. And what then, are these occupations that continue to draw people away from the local colleges?

Well, for starters, they all possess certain traits which can (and do), result in both high-paying positions and above average, job security.

Among the most popular of these are the following:

(a) Computer Repair Technician—currently the demand for such workers exceeds the present-day supply, and which many industrial planners recognize must certainly increase, in order to keep pace with the nations growing economy. In most cases, successfully completing a two-year program in computer repair, will be adequate enough for most students to find immediate employment, upon graduation. Even a six-month training certificate (although quite expensive to obtain), will also offer you the opportunity to work in this field. Likewise, an Associates Degree in either Electronics or Computer Technology will help to open the way for you with further opportunities within the computer industry.

(b) Various Craftsmen of all trades can earn an excellent income, while administering their own particular abilities. So think plumbers, electricians, hospital workers, veterinarians, and web-designers and you have some of the most in-demand professions now sought by todays employers. So here again, two-years (or less) of successful completion of a vocational education, will likely net you both continuing employment, as well as earning above average wages. Ironically, if your looking for either professional glamor or popular recognition, some public perceptions of the various trades tends to view such vocations as being less desirable, and thus they fail to emphasize the increasing demand (and pay) for such tradesmen. Now if you believe that the so called 'new economy' might somehow replace those vocations, then just look at the Department of Labor statistics for any one of them. In practically, every instance a worker shortage is forecast. So if a four-year college degree is not of any interest to you, then consider a vocation—and then go about living happily (and prosperous) ever after.

(c) Health care workers—Here...I'm not talking about either the doctors and/or nurses, but rather the job opportunities which are available as an X-ray technician, a medical assistance, or even as a position in accounting and/or customer service. Consider this fact—America's population is currently in the retirement years of its baby booming years of 1946 thru 1960. This means that now (and in future years), more and more retirees will be demanding even greater hospital care, than ever before. What that means, is simply this: more hospital workers will be needed to support both the doctors and nurses, as they try to cope with that ever-increasing patient load. Now add in the on-going required treatment of many clients for such ills as cancer and heart disease and it soon becomes apparent, that this field will only grow, in the immediate future.

So what type of training is really necessary for these positions? Well, like the other previous noted vocations, two-years or less in a related certified program, should normally be adequate enough, in order for someone to obtain employment here. And even though some localities may require a license for certain vocations, even that is fairly easy to obtain, once you acquire the professional knowledge and confidence towards making it happen. Of course, in addition to receiving your academic credential, you will also be receiving some 'on-the-job' training as well

To sum it all up, there are today, many high paying vocational positions which are available to anyone, who is qualified (either through education or experience), and who desires an occupation, to which no degree is either demanded—or is even necessary.

R.O.T.C. (Reserve Officers Training Corp)

During the Vietnam War, this alternative to a traditional college education was often criticized, primarily as a result of its direct connection to the military. Since that time however, thousands of military 'career minded' students have embraced the opportunity to get a post-secondary education, within the esteem realm of performing military service for their country. Here's how the program works: The various branches of the armed services offer a merit-based scholarship (up to $16,000) every year, thru various colleges and universities located throughout the country. Accordingly, those who are accepted into such programs, must also attend designated classes offered by the military. Upon graduation, the 'student' is then required to serve four-years as an active-duty officer in whichever branch sponsored that individuals education.

It should be noted here, that getting a scholarship from the R.O.T.C. program is very difficult, since the pool of applicants far outweighs the money that is currently available. Still, certain professions are given 'top-priority' consideration, when such awards are granted. Specifically, such areas of study are: nursing, business, science, and of course, engineering. So if your interests leaned towards one of those areas, and you would also like to serve your country while practicing it, then be sure to investigate the opportunities that are routinely available within the prestigious R.O.T.C. program

Americorps—is a federal funded program that combines both work and study functions, via some 450 national service programs. By mainly volunteering to serve up to two years in their community, (a one-year minimum of service is required) applicants can now earn vouchers for college in the amount of $4,725 per year. Conversely, if the volunteer decided to serve part-time (900 hours), he would receive only half that amount ($2,362.50). There are of course, numerous occupations which are available to those interested in such a program: educational opportunities, human services, environmental science work, public safety programs, and even some business related openings. In addition to these earned school 'vouchers', the volunteer is also paid a small weekly allowance of about $150. However, two important points are to be noted here: first, you will still be responsible for both your own housing and food expenses, and second, you clearly might be better off working at a regular job, where the wages are likely to be more than the small amount of pay thats currently available to you via the AmeriCorps program. It is also worth mentioning that even graduate students can apply and serve in that program as well.

An additional Americorps entity is simply called the National Civilian Corps(NCC). However, this 'junior' version of the mainstream Americorps program restricts the service thats traditionally required to those between the ages of 18-24 , as part-time service is not allowed under its charter. In addition, unlike its senior parent, the NCC does provide dormitory-style housing (and meals) on those few campuses, which participate in its program.

Clearly, either program will give you the opportunity to explore a future career, without your having much experience in that particular field. One final note: a full year of service in the 'junior' version of Americorps amounts to just ten months (not 12), and also includes health insurance coverage, as well.

Chapter 15

▼

CLOTHING COSTS—Revealing the naked truth!

Flip through the pages of most magazines, and your likely to find several advertisements hawking the advantages for buying upscale priced clothing. You know the names—Calvin Klein, Gloria Vanderbilt, and even Levi's 'upscale-priced' clothing attire. Yet, often times the quality that's found behind these designer label leaves one to question, if the premium price commanded for such names is truly worth the cost. Bottom line: Consumers would be wise to inspect each piece of such expensive clothing themselves, rather than depending solely on the designers name attached to it.

Specifically, that means to look for such important traits as these:

—Stitching—Check to see if it is tightly stitched together for maximum strength—or is it sewn several spaces apart where it can easily become unravel from mainly repeated washings?

—Seam Alignment—If you ever bought a pair of pants that were the correct size, yet still felt uncomfortable, then chances are the seams did not line up correctly. This basically is the result of poor quality control within the manufacturing process. Accordingly, this defect can also give an improper fit if the seams are misaligned by more than a quarter of an inch.

—Thickness of material—Want an idea of how durable a piece of clothing is likely to be? If so, there are two ways to determine that: First, hold the item up to the light. If you can easily see through it, that usually means the fabric itself is quite thin, and thus is likely to be non-durable after only just a few months of routine wear. Second—now feel the fabric. If it seems thick—like flannel, its very likely to be a better value than an ordinary weaved cotton might be. However, always keep in mind, the purpose for which your buying the item. For example, in July, you want a lighter weave material in order to benefit from the cooling effect of the summer breeze. Conversely, you would then want a thicker cotton flannel during the colder months, in order stay warm from the often times, bitter cold.

Color—believe it or not, certain colors have the capacity to either retain or reflect heat. Dark colors such as black will keep the heat close to the body, mainly from its absorption of energy from both your body and the outside elements, like the sun. Of course, if you've ever worn a black shirt during July, you know this to be true. Accordingly, lighter colors, especially white, will reflect lots of heat, thus making for a cooling effect. Likewise, this color principle also extends itself to many other consumer items also—(ie housing and our automobiles). Is it any wonder then, why many of the houses in southern Europe/and America, are today painted white? Answer: It is primarily used as a way to cut down on the homes summer cooling costs. Still other colors in the hue spectrum can be either absorbers or reflectors of heat, simply by the amount (and intensity) of the color, thats incorporated in the fabric. For example, a lighter shade of green will feel cooler, than one thats very dark. Naturally, most people will want a wardrobe consisting of both shades, simply to adjust for the various seasons of the year.

Retailers Store Policy—Sure you can by a designer label item at many upscale locations, but what if that stores return policy limits any return to say 30 days? If thats the case, then not only will you likely have paid a premium price for questionable quality, but now you will also need to buy another item to replace it, thus increasing your overall costs for that product. And if your thinking of returning the item directly to the manufacturer? Well, think again, since often times, the cost and trouble of that option, (i.e. shipping costs, obtaining 'advanced' return authorization (in writing) from the manufacturer,and/or following precise packaging instructions), hardly makes the return worth the extra bother. So to avoid putting yourself in such a costly and time consuming situation, always find out in advance, what the retailers return policy is. Needless to say, the longer it is, the better it is—for you!

Location, Location, and Location—yes, I know, those are the three points one should consider when buying real estate. Well, guess what—it also applies to the retailer when you buy clothing. Sure, you can buy a shirt at some 'out of town' location, but even if the store has a liberal return policy, that won't do you much good, if you can't return it there, because of the travel distance involved. So always look to a national chain retailer if possible. That way, even though you purchased the item from a different location, a local branch of that store, will often times, also honor its warranty. Of course, an exception to this rule, might be made when buying clothes while on vacation in a tax-free state. Granted, you'll be taking a risk in buying an independent (i.e. unknown) label from possibly an unknown retailer as well, yet if you know what to look for when buying clothing, (as previously mentioned), you will then likely be getting get a good deal—and for a good deal less!

House Brands—are even better quality than some of the more famous national brand names. It's true—in various consumer magazines, test performed on numerous clothing articles, showed that not only was the house brand sometimes less costly, but also that it was actually better made as well. What's somewhat ironic however, is the fact that the manufacturer for some of these same competing brands is actually made by the national brand leader. So why then is there a difference in price and/or quality? Well, in most cases, its because the wholesale manufacturer merely produces the product from the specifications of the retailer, rather than selling its own model directly to such national chain stores.

A retailer will do this for two reasons: First, he knows that the stores name and image is an important advertising trait, which in fact, relates directly to the consumers own idea of 'value pricing'. Thus, if a customer sees both value and quality, he most likely will buy many other store-brand products from that store, as well. So its not just one item which the retailer is selling, when it puts its own name on an item. In fact, its quite likely to be several hundred items over the years. In addition, by producing the item according to their own market research and industry insight, home brand retailers can turn a formerly unknown name into a national brand, while giving the consumer true value for the money. And that of course, is whats become known as a 'win-win' situation. The second reason for maintaining control over its brand name, lies in the stores own financial clout towards getting the best price possible from its various manufacturers, so as to pass along the savings to the consumer—and thus to increase its own sales (and profit) volume. The end result, simply means good value to the customer, more competition in the marketplace, and the build up of customer loyalty towards a particular house-brand name.

Yet price and quality are not the only criteria, you need to be aware of when buying items from these stores. A liberal return policy can be just as beneficial to you, as the initial sale was for that store. There's also another benefit in buying clothes from a national retail store—which also has a catalog sales department. For here's a little known secret, you'll certainly appreciate. Once you purchase any item from its catalog, you will also likely receive an advance sales notice via the mail, plus a coupon (10-25% discount value), which is usable even on its then-current sale prices. The bottom line: Check out your local mass retailer and then be prepared to get both value and quality on its merchandise.

Shipping and Handling Fees = the TRUE price of the product Although its possible to get a great price on many catalog items, its also just as easy to be ripped off, once the so called shipping and handling fees are added into that items final price. In fact, it sometimes happens that those charges will often exceed those on the item itself. But shrewd consumers can take steps to minimize those costs. First and foremost, add in the shipping cost to the items final price, to determine which is the better buy—retail or catalog. Also, if you are ordering several items at the same time, your shipping costs will likely be much less per each item ordered— which, in effect can easily mean big savings overall, to your true 'bottom line' price. And finally, remember those 'extra savings' mail coupons of 10-25%, that were mentioned earlier? Well simply consider them to be an 'indirect' payment which can be used towards reducing those 'necessary' high shipping charges. And speaking of extra charges, consider this—if you order an item from another state, which does not have a physical presence in your state, you can avoid paying the state sales tax all together. For example, if you order $1000 worth of goods, and your state/local sales tax is 8.25%, you've just pocketed $82.50. Not bad, considering all you had to do was to simply place a (toll-free) phone call, in order to have the item shipped. Of course, you'd need to deduct the shipping charges from that $82.50, but if you follow the preceding advice, your savings will amount to some serious money being either spent (or invested)—for your future!

CLEARANCE VS SALES ITEMS—Too often, consumers mistakenly assume that just because an item is advertised as being on-sale, it is in fact a bargain. This is simply not true—especially when you see advertisements that state such high discounts as 80%. Now if you've ever look closely at its former selling price, chances are you'll discover that it was a grossly overpriced item to begin with. And by how much you might wonder? Well, try 150%—or more. I mean think about it, how could a store stay in business while giving up such large discounts, as 80% off? The answer lies in the fact, that the original prices are normally raised very high, in order to hopefully maximize the stores profits margin. However, whenever the consumer rejects those premium costs, soon thereafter, the ON SALE signs immediately began to appear. Bottom line: always ask yourself this simple question—if the ad says its 50% off—what was the original price ? Once you know this information, you'll easily see thru the advertising ploy of the many 'ON SALE' items. However, if you discover that the regular retail price is somewhat average (to other retailers,) and then you spot a 'big' discount, then by all means, you'd want to take advantage of it. The bottom line is simply this—know your prices before you leap for their ON SALE advertisements.

CLEARANCE items are usually a 'true sale' opportunity for saving some big bucks in todays marketplace. Basically, these are items that for one reason or another, are no longer in large enough demand by the consumer, for keeping them on the retailers store shelf, and as a result 'out they go' at wholesale prices. Specifically, such items would likely be the so-called 'fad' items, (ie out of style clothing, unpopular colors, or even some unusual sizes. Of course, you won't find very many newspaper advertisements for clearance items, primarily because the available selection is usually limited to stock on hand. Yet, just about every retailer today has such clearance items year round. As such, these items can usually be found in an obscure section (i.e. the far corner of the clothing department) of many stores. Yet, it is here, that you'll discover the real value, in clothing. For here is also where you'll find that original priced item of $50, now selling for $5—or many times, even less.

Now when shopping for clothing, the best time to look for such deals is usually after the holidays, (i.e. during the month of February). Since this is the time when retailers have tried to unload their after Christmas merchandise thru sales in January, yet are still saddled with last years apparel 'losers'. Their solution—to sell it at any reasonable price—rather than having it take up valuable shelf space, thats already allotted for the incoming Spring line of clothing. Clearly, such 'super' deals on these clearance items can be had, for anyone who wants to keep aware of when certain clothing seasons end—and thus, when the real markdowns begin.

An example of this: would be buying your swimwear in August (in fact, most retailers consider July 4th to be the high sales point for such items). They know from experience that if most consumers have not bought that item by that date, then chances are they are unlikely do so, after then. (At least in not enough numbers, to justify the on-going allocation of valuable shelf space, for such seasonal wear). Bottom line: you get to buy some seasonal wear at about 90% discount—and once again proving that the consumer is still king, even in todays 'new' economy.

Now heres another outlet for 'everyday' clearance items—the factory outlet. In this instance, some items are likely to have a minor flaw and as such, are offered to the public at a substantial discount. At these locations, you will seldom see the word 'SALE' on their merchandise. Yet you can be quite certain that the discount is real and that there will NOT be any type of return warranty on such items.

Still, if you know what to look for, (i.e. quality) this is one of the best places for getting the most value for your clothing dollar. You can find these local factory outlets simply by looking in the yellow pages, under the heading of 'Outlets'. Just don't expect a retail-store layout of its merchandise, but rather one of concrete floors and hand-written signs which simply state those unbelievable discounts. Thus if your really interested in saving money, then the factory outlet is certainly one additional source, which you should always consider.

Still another type of 'factory outlet', now also appears at various shopping malls. However, from my own experience, I've found such items there to be less than ideal (pricewise, that is), when compared to many of the nearby stores that often carry the same item, at an even greater discount. Always remember, that the cost of real estate plays a big role in determining what the price of any item will cost the consumer. Accordingly, a cluster of such outlets found together in a mall, translates into some very high overhead. At least, that holds true when their compared to those factory manufacturing sites, which often has no additional 'on-site' costs to pass along to the consumer. In effect, this makes for the better 'value buy', between those two types of factory outlets.

It should be noted however, that many of the mall factory outlets do, in fact offer a money-back guarantee—which is an important point for any consumer to always consider, before parting with his hard-earned dollars! So always check them both out, since your certain to find what your looking for at a cost that should impress just about anyone...especially among those who are also thrift oriented.

ARMY-NAVY SURPLUS STORES

To most of the buying public, the idea of shopping at the local ARMY-NAVY surplus store, conjures up an image of outdated, heavily worn, and over-priced clothing attire, that caters mostly to former military personnel.

Yet for the American consumer, nothing could be further from the truth. Sure many of our former soldiers shop here, but so do many other folks. And the reasons are quite simple. First, there is the clothing 'quality' factor, that still pertains to the majority of such everyday (and basic) items as wool jackets, cotton sweaters, khaki pants, and even leather boots. In fact, these are the same quality of goods that still clothe todays military troops, all over the world,—and in all variations of climate, as well. And even though, some of the 'surplus' clothing here is used, much of it is not. Instead you'll likely find items that either have a slight flaw, or more than likely, are simply production 'over-runs' of the manufacturing process.

So if you think you can't find a good buy here, then consider the following: as a form of 'de facto' value:

—100% all cotton tee-shirts at 3 for $5

—All wool pants going for $20—vs. $75 (or more) from several of the major retailers

—Leather boots at just $25—which is a mere fraction of what a pair of quality made hiking boots would cost elsewhere.

Or how about a heavy-duty canvas tent, which is ideal for camping out in. Its palty price…under $150—vs a lesser quality made synthetic tent, thats purchased from a retailer at three times the price. I don't know about you, but the last time I found such well-made (yet inexpensive) items, was at a DOD (Department of Defense) surplus auction, which was sometime back in 1977. However, in recent years, the items that became available thru DOD, were clearly no longer the value they once were.

Also keep another consideration in mind, when shopping at your local ARMY-NAVY store. And that is, the fact that any manufacturer who gets a contract from the government to produce such clothing items, must adhere to the very strict specifications that are required for clothing items issued by the US government. Accordingly, this is quality made clothing that is sold to the American public at a very reasonable price.

Of course, there are also a few items sold here, that are both price and quality competitive with your that local retail 'specialty' store. This is especially true, when it comes to such seasonal items as camping gear in July, or ski equipment during January.

Often times, the Army-Navy surplus stores will find it very hard to compete with a specialty-type store, since many such national retailers will have a promotional incentive (via the manufacturer), to move their product during the identified historical period of high-demand. Of course, such heavily promoted items will also be a very high quality as well. So once you add in the various nationally known-brand labels to that 'on-sale' promotional 'mix', you can then understand why some surplus stores could use a lot more customers year-round, than what they normally get. Yet, for those 'in the know', the ARMY-NAVY stores can be a true bargain, to anyone who once again, knows what to look for in well-made clothing items.

Somewhat ironically perhaps, the so called 'Age of Aquarius' of the early 1970's saw many of the 'counter-culture' generation, buy their clothes exclusively from these surplus stores—and nowhere else. I clearly remember, one news article that, explained the obsession to shop there, as the publics desire for a 'return to basics' mentality. Well, whatever it was, that 'trend' also soon faded. As a result, the prices have come down, even while the advertising of such stores remains minuscule, (at least, when compared to most retail stores), while the quality of the goods sold there has never been higher. If that sounds like a 'Best Buy'…(it is!), then by all means be sure to check it out. Just be certain to inspect the quality of all clothing items closely—and always try on the item before you purchase, to be sure that it fits properly. One final note: if you can't seem to locate a Army-Navy surplus store in your city, be sure to check out the Yellow Pages or go onto the web and do a search for ARMY-NAVY surplus stores!

THRIFT STORES

Just about every city today either has its own thrift style clothing store, or is close enough to another city that does. Although you can find various items (ie clocks, small appliances, TV sets, books, records,—even computers) here as well, it is clearly the selection of clothing items, where you'll likely find the best deals.

In fact, one of the best ways to buy designer-brand clothing cheaply is to simply shop the thrift stores. Basically, these are the various 'charities' stores like Goodwill, St. Paul and the Salvation Army.

Their locations tend to always have a constant variety of the basic lines of merchandise, which is derived from a public, who is only too happy to donate such items, which are no longer needed by them. This results equates to a 'win-win' situation for both the giver and the receiver, with the former getting a year-end tax write off, and the charity getting some good to excellent quality clothing thats been donated for free.

It should also be noted here, that the old image of a pile of wrinkled clothes laying unsorted on some creaky table in a dusty store, is now a thing of the past. For if you have not visited, a thrift store lately, I can assure you that its definitely worth your time (and savings) to do so.

In most instances, this is what you'll find:

—Piped in overhead music being played while you look about

—Racks of clothing that are neatly placed on racks, (but unfortunately are also NOT labeled according to the size).

—Shoes which are displayed on a shelf, in much the same way, that you'd likely find that item to be presented in a major retail store

—Accessories (like ties and belts) positioned next to shirts and slacks, so as to make it easy for the customer to match his clothing selection

—And lastly, one of the best features of all—a fitting room.

In fact, you can make that several fitting rooms (in order to avoid having to wait). Which is just another way these stores are appealing to todays value-conscious consumer. OK…OK, I know, your probably somewhat curious about the thrifts store policy on returns.

Well you can relax, because most of them have either a 30 day money-back guarantee or a compatible replacement on certain items. As is the case with any store, you obviously will want to know what that policy is before you make a purchase there. Yeah…ok, but what about when they do not have the item you want? No-o-o-o problem—simply ask the clerk (or store manager) if he expects to receive such an item within the next few days. Although it might be difficult for the him to know such information, these managers will usually have a good grasp (from previous experience) on what items are likely to show up on their shelves over the next few days (and/or weeks). Better yet, many of them are also likely to know if one of the other nearby branches of that store, might possibly have the item in question.

So, if what your looking for is important enough for you to search it out, there are clear ways to find it via assistance from your local thrift store. One more point to consider: donating your old clothes (and other items) to a charity, helps fund their various self-help programs. So by shopping there you are not only helping yourself in getting a good deal but are also helping many others find employment as well.

Flea Markets—Do people really buy clothes there?

Of course they do—along with many other items as well. Clothing however, is only a small part of the overall sales, that is conducted at such events. Since many of the sellers there have acquired clothing stock either thru a block sale (ie from a 'going out of business' store) or even from their own closets at home, the usual variety of clothing goods here is rather small. Still, if your already there anyway, it's always wise to check out what's available, since many times, you'll see a real 'find', of which, the seller is simply unaware of that items 'true value'. A case in point—I recently visited a flea market, where the vendor was hawking hand-crafted belts, silver-embossed bolo ties, and all wool sport jackets. Each of these items would have easily cost twice as much at a local retail shop, yet the seller was clearly far more interested in selling his other goods (which were mostly higher-priced electronic goods), so he sold the clothing items for basically what the buyers had offered him.

There are however two negatives, in buying clothing items here. First...unlike the preceding mentioned stores, any clothing purchased here is clearly sold 'as is'. In other words, no guarantee—no warranty, and no returns allowed. Yet thats really not a problem if you know what to look for quality wise, and your also certain that the size is correct. For instance, with a sports jacket, you can simply try it on—right then and there. But with a pair of pants, well eh...no...not really. So you just might want to pass on that item. The bottom line then is simply this—if you think the 'low' price is right to the item's quality, size, style and appropriate function, then by all means buy it,—even without that much valued (and cherished) return guarantee. The second negative presented when buying at a flea market is one that many consumers are surprised to discover: many of the sellers don't accept anything but cash for their goods-no not even so much as a personal check. Over the years, I've seen many vendors forfeit a sale, simply because they would not accept either a local check or a even a credit card for their goods. Since many of these sellers are often times 'here today and gone tomorrow', its somewhat understandable, that if a check bounces they might need to spend a lot of time and effort trying to get paid for what they had already sold. Now so far as the absence of any credit card acceptance goes, many of the sellers, have told me that they simply don't want to pay the added cost to the credit card companies (usually about 4%) for the processing of such cards. Thus cash is king at such places, and judging from the crowds at almost all of them, that's the way it's like to stay in the future as well.

Hospital Gift Shops—I'll bet this money-saving 'retailer' comes somewhat of a surprise to you. I know it did for me, when I first discover these thrift-stores, just several years ago. Now you won't find a huge—or even a big selection here, but you will find some basic clothing items like dress shirts and slacks, athletic shoes, and even some pajamas and bathrobes. What surprised me the most however was the reasonable prices on many of those items. In fact, several of their prices were even quite competitive with some recent sales from many of the local retailers. So why did that surprise me? Well first of all, its a known fact, that anytime you have a 'captive' audience (ie little or no competition to challenge you), you can pretty much get away with charging any price that the customer will obviously need to pay, if he simply needs your product. Think for a moment of that lonely cartwheel vendor selling suntan lotion and sunglasses on the beach in July, and where his only real competition is located maybe half a mile away. For even though his prices seem high, if the public want those items, they'll either gladly (or reluctantly) pay his price.

End of story.

So why then doesn't the hospital gift shop charge higher prices? My guess is that they simply want to conduct a casual business that is convenient for the visiting public and to its patients as well—and on both counts, they seemed to have done exactly that.

Still returning goods at these facilities can vary quite a bit however. As a few will usually give the customer a week or even a month to return the item, before giving the appropriate credit or refund. While still others state flatly that 'ALL SALES ARE FINAL'. So once again, it pays to be aware of not only the price/quality aspect of the sale, but the vendors so-called 'customer-friendly' policy as well. As with all of the preceding clothing stores (outlets/surplus/flea markets), this type of retailer also has some 'negatives' that you clearly need to consider—namely, its 'operating'—eh...(no pun intended), I better make that its opened hours. On occasion I've been to some hospitals where the gift shop was only open for a few hours a day, and/or was usually closed on the weekend, (when most of its customers would likely be there). A few were even closed when its limited staff went to lunch.

So if you plan on buying clothes from this retailer, be certain you know its hours—especially if you ever need to return something. Other wise, you could end up making several unnecessary trips, and thus negate any true savings you might have acquired from buying there.

Epilogue

▼

Some final thoughts to consider

At the beginning of this book, I stated that by the time you'd finish reading 'Bonanza Bits', you would be a much wiser consumer. Accordingly, it is still my firm belief that once you begin to practice many of the suggestions I've offered here, you too will agree, that consumer education (rather than protection) is the real key to getting control of ones own spending, and buying/saving habits.

By now, you should have also realized that it is not really 'rocket-science' theory, that says by spending less, you will in fact have more dollars to spend (or invest—which is even more beneficial), for those other items, you also want, but don't honestly believe you can now afford. Quite simply though, it all comes down to making sound (priority) choices, in an other-wise, yet fiercely competitive marketplace. Always understand that it is you (rather than the merchants), who has the ultimate power to drastically change your own financial well-being. All it takes from you, is discipline, knowledge, and the will to just say 'no', to useless wants, and/or imagined needs.

Sure, it's ok, from time to time to splurge 'foolishly', if for no other reason than to just feel good about who you are—or to simply rewarding yourself. Just so long as you don't waste your money NORMALLY, (which truly is the financial red flag to watch out for), there is clearly no reason for you not to splurge on something special—every now and then. So relax—and enjoy, the 'ride' (and bounty) of life. After all the bottom line to better personal money management is simply control of both your wants and needs. For within each of us, is the power to choose. I've simply suggested that you use that 'power' wisely.

In this book, I have given numerous tips and advice for getting the best value of both your time and money. Yet like so many other things, no 'one size fits all' method can work for everyone, since personal taste is well…personal, and thus subject to the various likes and dislikes of every consumer. Yet, there still remains an underlying tradition to all our buying, saving and investing habits—and that is simply this: we all want value, (make that 'real value') for our hard-earned dollars. We also know that while advertising can inform us as to brand awareness, it can also sway us with a clever jingle or a sponsored endorsement from one of the many known national celebrities—and to be quite frank, that's just good business sense on the producers part. Conversely, we—the consumer needs to understand that it is us, each of us, to take the initiative to learn how to buy, compare products and then determine why and how one product is a better value than that of the competing item. But perhaps my most important 'bit' (pun intended) of advice to you is simply this: always recognize that whatever choice you make in the marketplace, you are, in fact the ultimate decision maker, and thus either the winner—or loser, of that choice. Tomorrow, you'll get yet another chance to decide where both your time and dollars will go. Hopefully, 'Bonanza Bits' has have helped you along in that endeavor!

About the Author

―――――――――▼―――――――――

Joseph R. Trudel has previously worked as both a Consumer Affairs Specialist and as an adult education instructor for Consumer Affairs in Northern California.

For several years he had previously published a regional consumer newsletter In addition his many consumer articles have appeared in various publications. Accordingly, he has also appeared on radio.

Mr. Trudel currently lives in Northern California, where he is a Consumer Affairs Consultant for both personal consulting and industrial consultation.